kie Sherman has been an adult education tutor and
er since the mid-1990s. After a zoology degree and
arch experience, she spent twelve years as a university
eers adviser and then ran her own business designing
√s. She has published over thirty books covering a wide
range of subjects, including one on how to find work
when you're over fifty.

Also available from How To Books

HOW TO WRITE AN IMPRESSIVE CV AND COVER LETTER
A comprehensive guide for the UK job seeker

Tracey Whitmore

WRITING A UCAS PERSONAL STATEMENT IN SEVEN EASY STEPS
A really useful guide to creating a successful personal statement

Julia Dolowicz

PSYCHOMETRIC TESTS FOR GRADUATES
Gain the confidence you need to excel at graduate-level
psychometric and management tests

Andrea Shavick

HOW TO SUCCEED AT INTERVIEWS

Dr Rob Yeung

HOW TO PASS PSYCHOMETRIC TESTS
This book gives you information, confidence and plenty of practice

Andrea Shavick

CREATING YOUR FIRST EVER CV IN SEVEN EASY STEPS
How to build a winning skills-based CV for the very first time

Julia Dolowicz

A GRADUATE GUIDE TO JOB HUNTING IN SEVEN EASY STEPS

*How to find your first job
after university*

Jackie Sherman

Constable & Robinson Ltd
55–56 Russell Square
London WC1B 4HP
www.constablerobinson.com

First published in the UK by How To Books,
an imprint of Constable & Robinson Ltd, 2014

A copy of the British Library Cataloguing in Publication Data
is available from the British Library

ISBN: 978-1-84528-522-7 (paperback)
ISBN: 978-1-84528-527-2 (ebook)

1 3 5 7 9 10 8 6 4 2

Printed and bound in the EU

CONTENTS

INTRODUCTION

The aim of this book is to show how, despite all the difficulties you may face, you can still be the one to get the job when you find yourself competing against other applicants. It will also give you ideas for earning a living or spending time after university in different but rewarding ways.

Nowadays, it is not that common to take a first job and then progress through the same organization or stay on a single career path until you retire. It is therefore important to think flexibly about work and try to make the most of every opportunity, even if you are forced to take a series of unsatisfactory or unrelated positions or have to endure long gaps between jobs.

Whatever you learned about yourself at school and university, you will learn much more when you are out in the work environment. Developing self-awareness is something to be embraced if you are to take control of your life.

GRADUATE JOBS

Graduates often feel cheated if they don't go into what they regard as a 'graduate job' directly after graduation, but if you are in that position it certainly doesn't mean that your three or four years at university are wasted.

1 Many jobs don't require a degree but are still satisfying, challenging, well paid or highly skilled – fulfilling some of the life ambitions you may have had as a university student. It

may not always be better to 'use' your degree if you find a far more satisfying and rewarding career in a non-graduate job or profession. And, of course, people become highly successful self-employed or freelance workers, or use their entrepreneurial skills irrespective of any educational qualifications.

2 It is quite common to take a more roundabout route through life and still end up making use of your degree or the capabilities and qualities gained at university. Statistically, according to the Higher Education Careers Service Unit (HECSU) and the Association of Graduate Careers Advisory Services (AGCAS), '*it is still more beneficial to be a graduate than not. Graduates earn more over time than non-graduates, and are less likely to be unemployed the longer they have been out of education. Although graduates may begin in non-graduate level employment six months after graduation, they move up the ladder relatively quickly, often within months.*'

3 It is a fact of life that there are more graduates looking for jobs than there are graduate jobs available. Because of this, employers can pick and choose which universities to visit, which qualifications and courses at these universities to target, and exactly what sort of people they want. It means that for many of you, it will be extremely difficult to compete, especially when you remember that you are also competing against last year's graduates who may have spent the previous year working and gaining valuable work-related skills and experience. Your best bet is not to fight them but join them: take on the best first job you can find and build up your own work-related skills and experiences over time.

Without giving up hope or turning your face against any attempt to gain a graduate job if it is what you want, you should realize that in the real world you may have to find alternatives and that doing so is not a failure on your part.

A STEP-BY-STEP APPROACH

If you are keen to gain a graduate job before you leave university, make sure you take full advantage of all the help you can get. By making use of your university careers service you can attend talks and workshops, get advice on your application forms and CV, take part in the milkround and recruitment fairs, apply at the right time and hope to be offered a job well before you graduate. You can also get advice from both within and outside your department about degree-related careers and follow up any contacts or visits that are offered.

If you are unlucky, if you don't want to apply for a standard graduate job or if you don't want to do anything about jobs until after you graduate, you will have to fall back on your own resources far more. This is where becoming familiar with the different avenues into work, identifying the various agencies that can help you and thinking laterally about different approaches to the work environment are all going to be far more important.

The good news is that in most places, graduates can continue to use many of the local university careers services once they have left their own institution.

Whichever route you take, all the issues are addressed in this book. In particular, the job-hunting process has been divided into seven steps to make the book simpler to use. This means that, if you are part-way through the process, you can concentrate on those steps that are the most appropriate. On the other hand, if the idea of finding work is completely new to you or you have been avoiding even thinking about it, you may prefer to take it one step at a time and work from Step 1 to Step 7

The steps are:

Step 1 – Discovering who you are – understand what motivates you and what you can offer.

Step 2 – Deciding what to do – as well as learning different techniques for making career decisions, whatever route you take into work you need to be aware of what lies behind your choice and how you can make the most of your capabilities.

Step 3 – Finding out about work – have a clear idea of what types of work are available and where you can find further information.

Step 4 – Getting ready to apply – learn how to analyse job advertisements and provide evidence of your suitability for the work.

Step 5 – Making applications – identify how and where to find vacancies, understand what employers need to know and learn how to present yourself in the most effective way

Step 6 – Going for interviews – be prepared for the range of interviews and tests you might face.

Step 7 – Changing direction – learn about other opportunities after university including self-employment or travelling overseas.

BEFORE YOU START

Whatever subject you have been studying, you have many different options when it comes to finding work after university. One important task is to identify your own motivation towards your degree subject; telling yourself that you should stick with it just because you have studied the subject for three or four years, and that not using it further would be 'a waste', is not a good enough reason.

Here are seven different approaches to life after university:

1   Go into a field that you may feel you have been training and preparing for during your time at university, such as medicine, architecture or law.

2   Find work as a specialist where your degree subject is either a necessary prerequisite or you will continue to work with the content or specific skills you have learned. For example, by teaching the subject, translating using your language skills, going into research or applying your knowledge in one of the associated professions.

3   Go into a related field, but one that people with other degrees can also enter. For example, a geologist could work as an environmental consultant or a mathematician might go into market research.

4   Use the transferable skills acquired through your studies and other areas of student life in a more general way. This could mean making the most of your communication, essay writing, research, analytical, critical thinking, numerical or planning abilities in jobs that are open to graduates of all disciplines or from a wide range of degree backgrounds.

5   Forget about the distinction between graduates and others and take a non-graduate job.

6   Change direction and follow an interest that you have discovered during your years at school or university that may be quite unrelated to your degree subject but in which you have discovered a keen interest, such as politics, journalism, the wine and spirits trade, acting, music, scriptwriting, the church or sport.

7   Set up your own business or become self-employed.

For example, a psychology graduate could:

1   Become a clinical or educational psychologist
2   Teach psychology in secondary school
3   Go into market research or human resources
4   Become a social worker, primary school teacher or banker
5   Become a customer service manager
6   Go into local radio as a presenter
7   Set up a catering business

And a chemistry graduate could:

1   Become an analytical chemist
2   Become a patent agent or Met Office scientist
3   Go into scientific journalism or medical sales
4   Go into accountancy or nursing
5   Become a cabin crew member or teaching assistant
6   Become a professional singer or rugby player
7   Make and sell home-made clothes or bags

Certain factors can influence your decision, so you may:

➢ Need to train further or take a conversion course before you can enter the workplace

➤ Find there are no jobs in your chosen field and have to look for alternative routes

➤ Start out and then have to backtrack or change direction

➤ Find it very difficult to decide exactly what you want to do

All these things are common, and you will find advice in this book that will help you move forward.

ACTIVITY 1

1 List the seven different approaches in your own order of priority. (Even if you haven't decided on a career, you probably know by now if you want to use your degree subject or not, and if you have self-employment in mind.) If you are completely undecided, you might like to put approaches 3, 4 and 5 together as one choice.

2 Taking your first choice, note down up to four barriers or obstacles that might stand in your way.

Barriers to job-hunting success

Some barriers can be harder to overcome than others, and they may include:

➤ Difficulties in travelling to the workplace or even to interviews

➤ Commitments that mean you cannot leave home even though your preferred type of work is not available in your area

➤ Not having certain relevant skills or experience

➤ Being limited by disabilities or physical characteristics, e.g. poor eyesight

➤ Poor English or communication skills

➤ Being unable to take a conversion or further training course because of financial constraints

➢ Lacking the motivation or knowledge about how to get started

➢ Not knowing what jobs you could do using your degree or particular interests or skills

➢ Fear of being trapped in a low-skilled job, e.g. secretary or shelf-stacker

If you have identified one or more obstacles, there are several ways to approach them, in conjunction with working through this book:

▪ Share them with others who may have a solution (e.g. they might offer a loan, a lift or help caring for a child or other dependant)

▪ Discuss them with staff in the university careers service, Citizens Advice Bureau or Jobcentre Plus, as they may know of grants, awards or other sources of help

▪ Identify routes towards your career objective and start at a lower point, e.g. part-time casual work for experience, a self-help book or free online course to develop skills or gain qualifications etc.

▪ Work round them by identifying alternative careers that might be equally satisfying but that do not require you to leave home or pay for training

▪ Do something about them, e.g. if there are skills you can improve, find out about local courses or tuition or be more proactive, for example by offering something in exchange for private lessons from a local postgraduate

▪ Forget the myths about 'never train as a secretary' etc. No one can trap you unless you limit your own horizons. Use each job or skill as a stepping stone, add it to your CV, but continue to aim higher. (Does a driving licence limit you to truck driving or taxi jobs?)

▪ If work is not available locally, a common alternative nowadays is self-employment. This may be temporary or could turn into a permanent choice and can range from web design to dog walking, music tuition or cake making. See Step 7 for further information.

BEFORE YOU LEAVE UNIVERSITY

There is nothing worse than discovering, too late, that you could have helped yourself gain a better job, learn more about yourself in relation to work or become more attractive to employers, if you had made certain decisions during your time at university. If you are still a student (or if you have left but have the time on your hands) here are a few things you might be able to fit in that will definitely help in your job search:

Identify and fill your knowledge gaps

■ Employers will expect you to have done your homework, and this is also vital if you are to make the right decisions. So what can you do to find out more about the industrial sector, type of work or actual employers that attract you? As well as reading any literature and browsing the internet, try to find time to talk to people doing the work, or organize visits, work experience, shadowing or even a spell of voluntary work. For example:

a   Interested in nursing, social work, teaching or care? Volunteer at a hospital, youth club, nursery, school, soup kitchen or care home, shadow a social worker or visit as many institutions as you can.

b   Thinking about the oil industry? Find out if there are any open days to go to, family members who may know contacts you could talk to, visit a refinery or shadow an intern for a day, e.g. as currently offered by BP

> ### EXAMPLE
>
> This is what one student wrote about the experience: 'During this day we discussed what it's like to work at BP, went into a lot of detail about his project, met everyone in his office and attended presentations on other people's projects. A really enjoyable day. A quick taste into life at BP spent talking to friendly people and stretching your knowledge on your subject.'

c   Journalism appeals? If you cannot get work on a student publication, try writing about events or reviews for any online magazines, set up a blog or try to get work experience at your local paper.

d   Think you might want to be an art historian? Go to auctions and galleries, talk to members of staff in antique shops and museums and find work experience as a porter or in the office of an auction house.

As important – use the time to explore whether a particular type of work is actually right for you. If you disliked the activities or environment you experienced through work shadowing, volunteering or visiting, you have time to target a different career.

Making the most of your leisure time

If you spent your first two years simply socializing or reading books alone in your room, now is the time to join a few clubs. Most universities have a wide range of activities to choose from so there really is no excuse for doing nothing concrete in the time you have left. Make sure they are interests you can enthuse about or show some expertise in and which will be worth writing about in that space on application forms asking what you have been doing in your spare time.

Leisure activities can also help develop specific work-related skills or some of the sought-after transferable skills like teamwork, leadership, communication or analytical skills. If you have an interest that complements a potential gap in other areas of your life (for example, if it involves writing and you are a mathematician, or it develops your numeracy skills and you are an arts or humanities student) it may even help overcome any negative stereotyping you might face.

Showing your best side

It is sometimes hard to find evidence of intangibles such as leadership qualities or that you are a team player, personable or can communicate well. Also, when you are competing against other graduates for a limited number of jobs, it is useful to have done that little bit more. If you can, use not only your leisure time but also other areas of student life to find a way to show you have these personal qualities. You will help make your applications stand out. For example:

➢ Become a student representative

➢ Set up a completely new club or society

➢ Take a role in your hall of residence or as an ambassador, welcoming new/overseas students

➢ Represent the university, e.g. in sports, debating or *University Challenge*

➢ Play an active part in student politics or union activities

➢ Take on a role of responsibility such as chairman, secretary or events organizer

➢ Find similar roles if you are involved in non-university leisure activities

➢ Become involved in community or town projects – voluntary work or campaigning, for example

➢ Show entrepreneurial spirit, e.g. set up a small business and sell things to other students, start a band or offer language, music, GCSE-related or English language tuition either on or off campus

This may be a minor point, but on some application forms there is a separate box for positions of responsibility. It is a good idea to aim to have something to write in every box.

Gaining relevant work skills or experience

The ideal candidate is someone who has already done the work or developed the necessary work-related skills, and if you are taking a vocational degree or have organized a built-in work placement, you will be doing this anyway. For other students, particularly if you are moving completely away from your degree subject or if the right job is likely to be highly competitive, you need to gain experience that will put you in a better position when it comes to applying for jobs. Certainly for many jobs where, in the past, inexperienced graduates could have joined a graduate training scheme direct from university, now there are so few vacancies you will find that having some relevant work experience can be vital.

EXAMPLE

According to a report from High Fliers Research Ltd, 'more than half of recruiters warn that graduates who have had no previous work experience at all are unlikely to be successful during the selection process and have little or no chance of receiving a job offer for their organization's graduate programmes'.

---

a Look out for internships and summer work programmes. More and more employers are offering work experience to students in the summer before their final year. These are different from the usual industrial placements offered to sandwich-course students, but if you manage to find a place on any of these schemes you will have a great advantage when it comes to applying for work at the same company (or similar businesses) when you graduate.

EXAMPLE

In 2013, Kellogg's was offering a six-week Summer Financial Internship, paying £15,000 pro rata, and the details included this statement: 'Every Kellogg's Summer Intern owns and completes a challenging, meaningful project that contributes to our business. Our Interns are coached by business and technical masters in their fields of expertise. During your time with us, you'll be building your network and expertise in a thriving environment of professional development and teamwork. If you impress us and we impress you, there may be opportunities for you to start your career with us after you graduate. If you join us as a Graduate then you will continue to grow and develop, whilst we support you to attain your CIMA Qualification. '

You may be surprised how many different companies and organizations offer relevant work experience via placements. For example, if you wanted experience in marketing, the following types of organization were offering opportunities in 2013:

Banks – Barclays, Nationwide
     and Lloyds
Pharmaceuticals – GSK and
     Proctor & Gamble

Telecoms – O2
Computing – HP
Paints – AkzoNobel
Cosmetics – L'Oréal

Food – Nestlé   Finance – American Express
Car rental – Enterprise   Fashion – Linda Farrow

EXAMPLE
Centrica ten-week summer placement
Locations: UK-wide. Accommodation provided locally
Salary: £14,000 pro rata

During your placement you'll work on real projects and undertake interesting and varied work that will make a real contribution to the business. You'll have the support of your colleagues, line manager and the Central Graduates team to ensure your placement is a success. We'll also endeavour to ensure you get to work in an area of the business that you are interested in. We can't always meet your aspirations but we will provide a challenging, hands-on experience to equip you with core skills that you can transfer to any workplace. Your placement will be in one of the following areas:

- Analyst
- Customer Operations
- Engineering
- Finance
- Human Resources
- Information Systems
- Marketing & Insight
- Subsurface

---

b   Build up a portfolio of activities through university life. For example, if you are interested in a career in fashion, get involved in design and fashion shows – either organize your own or build up contacts with organizers at your university or at a local arts college. If you want theatre administration work, take part in reviews or help behind the scenes either on campus or with a local amateur dramatics group. And if you are aiming for a computer games design career, join any gaming societies and get broader experience playing, reviewing or just chatting to other players.

c   Get a part-time or holiday job in the same sector or dealing with similar customers, products or services.

EXAMPLE

One graduate who is now a buyer for Oasis started her career as a Saturday shop assistant at Laura Ashley and after graduating became an assistant manager there.

---

d   Try to get a job that develops some relevant skills even in a different sphere. For example, if aiming for restaurant management, any cooking or food preparation job such as in a canteen or care home will be useful; if you want to organize adventure holidays, working at a local airport or living abroad for a while will provide valuable insights into the sector; and if going into production management, working under a manager in a different area will still help you identify good management practices.

e   If taking a gap year or travelling in the summer, think about the relevance of the countries and cities you could visit or jobs you might find before making final decisions. Write a journal, think about the culture and meet as many people as possible so you have lots to talk about and can make more informed comments about international affairs.

f   If there are no related jobs available, work experience or voluntary work will give you the same experience, help you make useful contacts and develop the same skills even though you won't be paid. If you can afford to spend only half a day per week or month as a volunteer, it is still far better than nothing. There are even online or home-based voluntary activities available. For example, to get proof reading experience, check text for Project Gutenberg (an organization that distributes free e-books to the general public) – see www.gutenberg.org/wiki/Gutenberg:Volunteering_for_Project_Gutenberg

Gaining transferable skills

Getting any job is better than no job, as it shows initiative and that you have the right work ethic. You will also learn things you cannot learn inside a university department. Here is a list of the most important employment skills and personal qualities identified in a survey of American employers:

- Communication skills
- Honesty/integrity
- Interpersonal skills (relates well to others)
- Motivation/initiative
- Strong work ethic
- Teamwork skills (works well with others)
- Computer skills
- Analytical skills
- Flexibility/adaptability
- Detail-oriented
- Organizational skills
- Leadership skills
- Self-confidence
- Friendly/outgoing personality
- Tactfulness
- Well-mannered/polite
- Creativity
- Entrepreneurial skills/risk-taker
- Sense of humour
- Bilingual skills

And here is a similar list produced by surveying UK employers:

- A positive attitude: a 'can do' approach
- Good work ethic
- Willingness to learn
- Self-reliance
- Good personal presentation
- Honesty and integrity
- Reliability
- Timekeeping and personal organization
- Team working, collaboration and cooperation

➢ Flexibility

➢ Commercial awareness and customer focus

➢ Communication skills – oral and written

➢ Numeracy

➢ Computer literacy/IT skills (nowadays, this will include an understanding of social media or blogging etc.)

By working through these lists, you should be able to identify which activities you have been involved in that can provide the evidence that you have such skills or traits. They could come from courses, examinations, work experience, leisure, school or college activities, through family or from other areas of your life.

ACTIVITY 2

1   Take three of the transferable skills listed above.

2   For each one, identify up to three different activities you have been involved in that demonstrate you have that skill or personal quality.

If you don't think you have done anything that would display such skills, try to find a way to provide the evidence before you leave. For example:

➢ Take a short course, e.g. in public speaking, a language or IT

➢ Work through a self-help book, e.g. on numeracy or business

➢ Get help from family or friends who may have valuable expertise they could pass on

➢ Get involved in home-based micro-volunteering activities (small projects that only need last from five minutes to half an hour). For example, there are many craft, computing, translating, answering questions, e-mentoring, writing, recording or other opportunities available – find out more at www.helpfromhome.org

➢ Find a way to develop concrete skills such as learning to drive (as this is helpful in some jobs or for just getting to work) or more specialist computing, social media or web-related skills, e.g. become familiar with Excel, SAGE, Photoshop, Illustrator, HTML, C++, ASP.Net, C# or JavaScript

➤ Try to get involved in a group project or help or cooperate with others in some tangible way and develop your leadership and/or teamwork skills

➤ Build the skills into a part-time job, e.g. try to gain more face-to-face customer contact, administration, database input, writing or speaking experience

➤ Join a club where you will need or can display the skill, e.g. become a member of a team, offer to be the finance officer or offer to take on the role of spokesperson etc.

➤ Take any job so that your referees will confirm good timekeeping, honesty, teamwork, work ethic, interpersonal skills, reliability and business understanding etc.

➤ To show self-reliance, try to ensure that you can talk about a self-directed project where you identified weaknesses or areas for improvement

➤ To show honesty and integrity, try to take on a role where you are handling money, dealing with confidential information, perhaps in a counselling or mentoring role, or keeping other people's personal data secure

Once you leave, you will never again have so many opportunities or time to experiment with work and leisure activities that are available during your university years.

STEP 1

DISCOVERING WHO YOU ARE

There are two major reasons for developing your self-awareness and building up a personal profile of your skills, interests, qualifications and experiences in relation to finding work. This activity will help you:

➢ Direct your efforts towards jobs in which you are likely to find the most satisfaction

➢ Provide evidence of your skills, abilities and interests to convince employers that you are the best candidate

Let us imagine that you can identify three different experiences:

1 **Gaining life-saving and swimming certificates**

   a   This tells you about a particular sporting interest and ability that you have and it may lead you to explore areas of work where confidence around water is important, e.g. lock keeping, merchant navy, leisure management, cruise ships, marine pilot, swimming instructor etc.

   b   When applying for jobs that require you to be a proficient swimmer, you have qualifications that demonstrate motivation and a measurable level of skill

2 **Working as a volunteer at a veterinary surgery**

   a   If you enjoyed the experience, it might indicate that you should look for jobs related to animals. If you disliked being in the surgery, but still enjoyed working with dogs, for example, you might be happier looking into dog walking, dog kennel management, dog training etc. rather than indoors work.

b It is clear evidence of motivation and experience of working with animals and you will have developed customer service, office and other work skills.

3 Taking a holiday job as a chalet helper at a ski resort

a If this confirmed that you particularly enjoy working abroad, in skiing and winter sports, cooking or making groups of strangers feel at home, it could be worth considering jobs such as working in the travel industry as a tour guide or overseas representative, becoming a sports instructor, or working in catering or the hospitality business.

b This work can provide evidence of a number of intangibles such as social skills, being able to work independently, confidence in foreign situations, as well as the actual skills involved in catering, winter sports or working with groups.

As you can see from these examples, discovering your personal traits and preparing an inventory of evidence can mean exploring a wide range of past experiences. It takes time to build up a really complete picture of what you can offer and what might motivate you towards or away from particular work activities, and it is also something that doesn't stop. Each new experience will throw new light on who you are.

For every activity you have been involved in, whether at school, university, at home, at work, alone, in a peer group or with your family, there are a number of questions you could ask yourself to help build up your self-knowledge. For example:

1 Why did you choose it?
2 What did you enjoy most about it?
3 What did you enjoy least?
4 What did you do well?

5   What did you do poorly or struggle with?
6   What would you do differently if you repeated the experience?
7   What was missing from the experience?

EXAMPLE

Here is how one biology graduate answered the questions in relation to her degree as a whole:

➢ Chose – one of her two best school subjects (the other was English). She was encouraged to go into science as there were more employment opportunities

➢ Enjoyed – writing essays and reading round the subject

➢ Disliked – practicals and fieldwork

➢ Did well at analysing information and presenting it in a summarized form

➢ Struggled in the first year as had to study physics and chemistry, which were her poorest subjects

➢ She would have thought more about which subject to study and might have preferred English

➢ There was too limited a choice of specialist options in the final year. She wasn't interested in any of them, chose one to start with and switched to another rather late. She did very poorly in it

*Despite these likes and dislikes, she still went into research but dropped out during her second year as practical work was not her strength.

STARTING THE PROCESS

Before taking a systematic approach to identifying your personal qualities, it is worth putting down on paper everything you can think of now that you feel sums you up. This will include:

➢ Skills – things you are good at

➢ Interests – things you enjoy or choose to do

➢ How you come across – how family and friends would sum you up

➢ Preferred environment

➢ Any goals, both short- and long-term

➢ Achievements, e.g. personal, at school, in work, at university

➢ Any 'dream' jobs or careers

➢ Other jobs you have considered

➢ Jobs you would dislike (with reasons)

➢ Obstacles that need to be overcome

Once it is all down in front of you, you can add to it as you work through the rest of the book. Ideally you will end up with a very complete picture of yourself that will inform your research and any choices you make.

ACTIVITY 3

1   Spend fifteen minutes or so putting down everything about yourself that might impact on your future career or next endeavour. Either produce lists or create a spidergram, where each new idea is linked by a line to a previous one. If you come to the end of a line of thought, start a new 'leg'.

2   Over the next few weeks or months, add extra ideas or thoughts to the page.

PERSONAL QUALITIES

Although sometimes hard to quantify, it helps to be able to identify your particular strengths and what you could bring to a job. One way is to identify your key personal qualities or traits.

Here are thirty examples of qualities that you might have and which may have more relevance in particular types of work:

Assertive	Enthusiastic	Patient
Charismatic	Flexible	Perceptive
Compassionate	Generous	Persistent
Confident	Honest	Punctual
Consistent	Kind	Self-motivated
Courageous	Knowledgeable	A sense of humour
Creative	Loyal	Tactful
Decisive	Methodical	Tolerant
Dependable	Modest	Unselfish
Empathetic	Organized	Wise

ACTIVITY 4

1 Pick out five qualities from the list that you feel you have.

2 Provide the justification for your choice, e.g. 'Honest – I always hand back change in shops if I am given too much and don't believe in telling lies.'

3 Pick out up to five that you feel you are lacking. Can you do anything about them?

SKILLS AND INTERESTS

It is obvious that you are more likely to succeed and be happy in work that you are capable of doing and that you enjoy. Identifying your skills and interests is an important task if you want some ideas for which careers or jobs might suit you best, and is also key when it comes to analysing potential vacancies that you might be applying for.

Skills list

A common way to help identify your abilities is to look through a list of skills and select any that appeal or that you feel you could offer. In reality, such lists are not a great deal of help in isolation as it usually depends on the context (for example, speaking to one person is very different to speaking to a hall of 500), but if you want to see what skills are possible, here is a list of more than 150.

Activating	Changing	Corresponding
Acquiring	Checking	Creating
Adapting	Classifying	Deciding
Adding	Cleaning	Delegating
Administering	Collating	Delivering
Advising	Collecting	Describing
Analysing	Combining	Designing
Appraising	Communicating	Detecting
Arranging	Comparing	Developing
Assembling	Compiling	Devising
Assigning	Completing	Diagnosing
Auditing	Computing	Directing
Building	Consolidating	Discussing
Buying	Constructing	Dispatching
Calculating	Consulting	Dividing
Calling	Contracting	Drafting
Caring	Contributing	Drawing

Driving	Keeping (records)	Reconciling
Editing	Leading	Recording
Enabling	Lecturing	Recruiting
Encouraging	Liaising	Reporting
Endorsing	Listening	Representing
Enforcing	Listing	Researching
Enlarging	Making	Resolving
Entertaining	Managing	Reviewing
Establishing	Measuring	Scheduling
Estimating	Memorizing	Searching
Evaluating	Mending	Securing
Examining	Modifying	Selecting
Experimenting	Monitoring	Selling
Explaining	Motivating	Serving
Familiarizing	Negotiating	Simplifying
Filing	Notifying	Solving
Forecasting	Obtaining	Sorting
Formulating	Operating	Speaking
Generating	(equipment)	Standardizing
Granting	Organizing	Stimulating
Growing	Performing	Stocking
Guiding	Persuading	Summarizing
Hiring	Planning	Supervising
Illustrating	Presenting	Supporting others
Improving	Preventing	Surveying
Informing	Problem-solving	Teaching
Initiating	Probing	Testing
Inputting	Programming	Training
Inspecting	Proof-reading	Transcribing
Instructing	Proposing	Translating
Interpreting	Providing	Updating
Interviewing	Questioning	Validating
Inventing	Rating	Verifying
Investigating	Reading	Watching
Judging	Recommending	Writing

As you can see, some of these can be linked fairly obviously to work activities and you should be able to decide if you have the skill or could enjoy tasks such as filing, editing, reporting, interviewing, illustrating, recruiting or supervising. Others are more difficult to place. For example, is there any specific job you can think of that requires preventing, watching, reconciling or providing – or can you remember times or places in your life where you have used these skills? Again, there are very few jobs that will not involve a large number of the skills listed at least at some time, particularly:

➤ Communicating (e.g. instructions, information, decisions)

➤ Writing (e.g. emails, memos, reports, adverts, instructions)

➤ Listening (e.g. to customers, to patients, to tapes, to your manager)

➤ Creating (e.g. art or craft items, a positive atmosphere, ideas, displays of work)

➤ Improving (e.g. original products, flavours, room arrangements, ways of working, training)

➤ Informing (e.g. staff, customers, clients, colleagues, the press, TV audiences)

➤ Solving (e.g. problems with time, timetables, staffing, deliveries, software etc.)

Categories

You may find it easier to identify your skills or interests by grouping them under different 'working with' categories. For example:

People – if you enjoy or feel you are particularly good at advising, listening, supporting, interviewing, persuading or managing.

Things – such as being good at constructing, operating, repairing, sorting or adapting.

Ideas – perhaps you are successful at evaluating, questioning, planning or presenting.

Artistic or creative concepts – you may have a natural leaning towards writing, painting, films, music or other arts or crafts.

ACTIVITY 5

1 Put the above four groupings in order of your own leanings or strengths.

2 Is there a more appropriate category you should add?

3 Put down four or five examples of successful and enjoyable activities in each of these categories, e.g. Creative – make your own clothes; People – persuading customers to buy your goods from a market stall.

4 Do you have a particularly strong interest or even an overriding passion that you want to follow through in a career?

Using your Curriculum Vitae

Another way to identify your capabilities and interests is to review as many activities as possible that you have ever been involved in. Wherever you have succeeded or particularly enjoyed yourself, recognizing the activity will help you draw up your own personal skill set. You will need to cover your time at school, college and university, in work, during leisure and family time and in lone pursuits.

Although brainstorming can be a good starting point, you can quickly run out of ideas as it is often hard to remember everything in detail, and even large chunks of time are likely to be missing.

By now, you will probably have at least started to produce a CV as details of your past experience will be needed when making job applications (see Step 5 for advice on how to set one out). It should provide a record of your education, training, work and possibly leisure activities and, depending on how it is organized, could present a chronological picture or put more emphasis on successes, attitudes, what you have to offer and your transferable skills.

Now every section will provide evidence of your abilities and interests, including:

- Qualifications such as GCSEs or certificates

- Subjects studied or courses attended that were not tested or examined, e.g. an introduction to the library classification system

- General skills, e.g. computing, driving, languages, music, craft, budgeting, organizing, planning etc.

- Work or leisure skills and interests such as working on the till, as a waitress, office filing, dealing with queries over the telephone, dancing, sign language or pottery

- Positions of responsibility (often indicating leadership skills), e.g. prefect, college representative, secretary of a committee or club, Scout leader

- Achievements or things you are proud of, such as setting up a new society, travelling solo across Europe, gaining promotion, voluntary work in the community or successfully fund-raising for a charity

Note that you need to identify interests as well as skills and experiences for true self-awareness, so it might be worth adding an 'Interests' section separately if you have not included one already.

Item	Good at	Poor at	Enjoy	Dislike
Mathematics		X		X
Writing	X		X	
Travelling			X	
Working with animals			X	
Languages	X		X	
Films			X	
Drawing	X			

FIGURE 1

You can then use it to note down activities that wouldn't necessarily be on a CV but that you should take account of in this exercise.

Assuming you are in your early twenties and not a mature student with many years of employment to explore, it will still take time to work through each section in detail but, if you do, you should find that it helps you identify key motivators and capabilities.

Applying the seven questions set out above, try to identify why you made your choices, what you enjoyed or disliked, what you did well or badly, what you would have done differently and if there was anything missing from the experience. At the same time, draw up a table (Figure 1) that lists the subjects or activities you have been involved in that you feel most strongly about. It could have the following six headings:

1 Good at – add an X if you were particularly successful in this
2 Poor at – add an X if this is something you failed or did badly
3 Enjoy – add an X if you feel very positive about it
4 Dislike – add an X if you do not want anything to do with this
5 Key requirement – add an X if you would ideally like this as part of your future work
6 Evidence – confirm to yourself that your feelings about subjects or activities are based on real experience and knowledge. This will also be valuable when you want to provide evidence of your personal abilities in job applications

Key requirement	Evidence
	Had to take GCSE twice
	Write fantasy stories in spare time
X	Loved my summer travelling
X	Volunteered at animal sanctuary for past three years
X	Taught myself French and Greek
	Go to the cinema at least once a week
	Building up a portfolio and taking evening class

Roles

A different approach is to think of yourself in terms of the roles you have played in life. These will be unofficial as well as official roles and could include:

➤ Family roles – daughter, brother, cousin, uncle

➤ Relationship roles – partner, friend, colleague, mentor

➤ Education roles – pupil, student, monitor, head girl, teacher/tutor

➤ Work roles – sales assistant, waiter, mechanic, web designer

➤ Social roles – chairperson, editor, carer, hospital visitor

➤ Hobbies roles – photographer, knitter, gardener, musician, IT expert, footballer

If you have time, think about yourself in every role you have identified to provide clues to your personality and interests. For example:

1 As a teacher helping your younger sister with her homework, what did you enjoy or dislike about the activity?

2 As the editor of the school magazine, what were the best and worst parts of the job?

3 As a member of the university rowing team, what were the highlights and were there any negative aspects?

4 As a friend at university, did friendships come easily or did you have to work at staying part of the group?

ACTIVITY 6

1 Identify four roles – each one from a different category.

2 Note down an experience you had in that role and what you liked or disliked about it.

3 If any clear patterns emerge, or you discover new things about yourself that could be relevant to future work, add them to the personal profile or spidergram you are building up.

Expertise

As well as skills and interests, you should also identify areas of expertise or any specialist knowledge that you have that you might want to build on in a future job.

ACTIVITY 7

1 Return to your CV or work through your education, training, work, leisure and other experiences.

2 Write down any knowledge areas you identify. For example, if you studied science, you may know something about scientific equipment, handling chemicals, logging data on a computer etc. If one of your hobbies is gardening, you might know about growing vegetables, tree pruning or landscaping.

3 When you have completed your list, prioritize your expertise so that you have five to ten areas that you are both knowledgeable and enthusiastic about.

VALUES AND NEEDS

Needs are those things that give you emotional security and satisfaction, such as having enough money to feed and clothe yourself. Values are the principles or standards by which you live your life and can also be identified as those things you would like to achieve or be known for, e.g. making people happy, improving the environment or creating beautiful things.

Many websites and books provide lists of values, so here are thirty examples:

Service	Accomplishment	Creativity
Participation	Orderliness	Adventure
Freedom	Integrity	Fairness
Excellence	Common sense	Challenge
Self-expression	Sensitivity	Dignity
Spirituality	Security	Caring
Enthusiasm	Equality	Friendship
Honesty	Achievement	Influence
Peace	Community	Acceptance
Risk-taking	Success	Reward

ACTIVITY 8

1 Look at the list and pick out the five values that are most important to you, or add others of your own.

2 Write down exactly what each value means to you. For example, you may interpret 'Reward' as financial, positive feedback, promotion or opportunities for growth and development.

3 How much would you want these values to feature in your future work?

Although your values are what drive you and determine how you approach life, you will find it hard to find a job that reflects them all, not least at the early stage of entering a career or starting work.

It is still important to recognize them; a mismatch between your values and those of your employing organization or line manager can cause unhappiness and stress and could even make you leave your job.

Here are a few examples of possible clashes:

- You are asked to carry out tasks that mean cheating or taking advantage of customers whereas you value honesty or integrity

- You are treated unfairly and your wages are cut when you don't feel it is justified but you value fairness

- You are promised promotion but it never materializes though you value fairness or reward or success

- You are poorly trained and then criticized for failures where you value accomplishment or creativity or fairness

- You are not provided with the proper tools and cannot get satisfaction from your work but you value creativity, excellence or accomplishment

- You are bullied and the management does nothing about it but you value integrity, equality or security

- You are pressured to keep quiet about health and safety infringements but you value honesty or integrity

- Your salary on promotion is much lower than you expected but you value reward or honesty or fairness

In the work situation, many people value similar things and most employers will tell you that, certainly for graduate-level jobs, that is what they try to offer. So most of us value a pleasant environment, autonomy to decide how to get on with the job, being treated fairly, variety in our work, recognition for work well done, support when we need it, opportunities for advancement, a chance to have fun and reasonable financial rewards. This is the ideal but, in most jobs, there are sure to be disappointing aspects that you just have to put up with.

The fact that many jobs do not provide all the things you might want is often irrelevant if it is the only job on offer, and most people can work round difficulties when they arise. So perhaps a more helpful way of looking at values is to discover where you would draw the line and turn down a job.

Would you take a job, for example, if it meant:

➤ Travelling away from home for several days at a time? Or do you value home and family life too highly?

➤ Working very unsociable hours? Or do you value seeing friends and family too highly?

➤ Working on your own most of the time? Or do you value companionship too highly?

➤ Having to experiment on animals? Or do you value animal welfare or the sanctity of life too highly?

➤ Working in a basement, cold laboratory, noisy factory or cramped office space? Or do you value a pleasant environment too highly?

➤ Having a long drive to and from work? Or do you value family time or a stress-free beginning and end of the day too highly?

➤ Being supervised at all times, with little opportunity to make decisions? Or do you value autonomy too highly?

➤ Having to move around a lot and carry out your work at a number of different locations? Or do you value stability and familiarity too highly?

➤ Needing to make a certain number of sales before you are paid commission? Or do you value financial security too highly?

➤ Working with ill or dying people? Or do you value avoiding unpleasantness or pain too highly?

➤ Not receiving any further training? Or do you value continuing education too highly?

➢ Working with people you don't particularly like, or who are all older or younger than you? Or do you value peer friendships too highly?

➢ Having to spend all day in front of a computer or on the telephone? Or do you value physical freedom or variety too highly?

➢ Having to meet tight deadlines or constantly feel under pressure? Or do you value a stress-free environment too highly?

➢ Having to keep meticulous records or do a great deal of paperwork? Or do you value avoiding boredom too highly?

It is often only when you are in a job that you can identify your key values and needs and what is wrong with the work, but if you look back over all your past activities, it might be possible to see what gave you the most or least satisfaction. It is important to take a note of anything that you feel would be impossible for you to put up with and also to analyse potential jobs very carefully, so that you can feel positive about what they would entail.

ACTIVITY 9

To help you identify your key values, carry out these three tasks:

1 Think of a time when you felt at your best or happiest. Write down what gave you that feeling expressed in terms of one or more values. Perhaps it was being creative, being praised or making other people happy.

2 Think of an incident where you got really annoyed or upset. What was the situation, and does it indicate any underlying values? For example, did someone treat you rudely, reject your views or show intolerance to others?

3 What couldn't you live without? Whether it is a person, thing or activity, try to identify what makes it so important. For example, do you value the peace and quiet when fishing, the exhilaration you feel when dancing or the companionship of a dog?

Life categories

A different approach is to divide your life into seven to ten categories. These will be personal to you but might include:

➢ Family   ➢ Health and fitness

➢ Relationships   ➢ Spirituality

➢ Leisure pursuits   ➢ Social life

➢ Finance   ➢ Work

➢ Environment   ➢ Contribution to society

For each category, try to identify your current or most recent satisfactions with it and what rating you would give it out of ten.

If you give any category a low score of zero to three, what is the reason and can you remember any times or situations when you would have given it a much higher rating? If you have rated a category between seven and ten, what has made you give it such a high score? Finally, if you have scored any category around five, what would have needed to happen to make you give it a higher score?

The answers will give you some clear pointers towards your values and needs.

For example, if you score low on 'social life' because you are living at home at the moment and few of your friends are around to go out with, and you would score your first or second year at university much higher, it could mean you value friendships highly, and/or need people of your own age around. You might want to find a job that is very sociable or which allows you to develop friendships – either with colleagues or customers/clients – easily. If you are in the same position but are quite content with your lack of a social life, it might be the case that you would be well suited to self-employment or jobs where you might need to spend a large amount of time on your own.

Again, if you rated your financial position very low because you couldn't spend on clothes or entertainment and all your high ratings depended on you having a fair amount of money in your pocket, it could indicate that one of your priorities is to earn a good wage or know you could do so in time. This could determine what types of career you should be considering. If having little money doesn't worry you, salary may be of minor importance when considering future careers.

ACTIVITY 10

1 Draw up a list of your own personal choice of category headings.

2 For each one, identify a situation that would justify a high score and another that would justify a low score.

3 To produce a record that you can refer to, set out your analysis in the form of the following table (Figure 2).

Category	Reasons for a High Score	Reasons for a Low Score
Finance and money	Having enough money so no need to worry about it, being able to spend on myself and friends	Worrying about it all the time, not feeling I can spend what I like
Health and fitness	Cycling – winning races, being at the peak of fitness, part of a team	When I broke my leg, felt left out, worthless, no fun, got seriously out of condition
Social life	Lots of friends within easy reach, always places to go with others	Being on my own, no one to have fun with, boredom
Environment	Love London or other big cities – always places to get to and things to do	Hate being stuck in a small village, nothing to do, everyone knows your business

FIGURE 2

WORKING CONDITIONS

If you ask people what they like or dislike about their work, they will often talk about the hours, the physical conditions, the pay, the people they have to deal with or the travel to work. These 'perks or peripherals' are what can make or break your enjoyment of your job and so are very important. Before actually accepting a job, you need to find the answers to any questions of this nature that you are concerned about. You will note that they are often closely related to your needs and values.

Here are some examples:

1   Where will you be based?
2   What will your starting salary be, and how does it increase?
3   What is your working environment like?
4   Is there much or any travel involved?
5   What are your hours, including any work at weekends?
6   Who will you be reporting to?
7   Is there a good induction training programme?
8   Is there any compulsory training?
9   What are your chances of internal promotion?
10 Is there a subsidized canteen or any staff facilities like a social club, gym or regular outings?
11 How many other people work at the same site?

One way to approach these questions is to group them into various categories such as:

Aspect	Examples
People to deal or work with	Customers Children, young people, patients or the elderly Colleagues of your own age On your own or very few other staff
Size of organization	Large, international Medium-sized Small

Aspect	Examples
Place you are based	Outside – on water, land, oil rig School, hospital, prison Office, laboratory or from your car Have to move to a strange town or overseas
Money	Highly paid Low pay Risky – commission and bonus-led
Hours you have to work	Nine to five Unsociable, often early or at weekends Night shifts Flexible
Training and development	On the job/in-house Go out to college Encouraged to develop new skills None
Travel	Main part of the job Work from home Some international travel Very little
Journey to work	Can walk Quite local and easy access Long or awkward journey
Perks	Discount on in-store purchases Canteen, gym, outings Medical insurance None
Promotion	Well structured Available to some Little opportunity
Day-to-day tasks	On the telephone or computer all day Heavy physical work Meetings and paperwork Using your hands
Work contract	Full-time, permanent Part-time or short-term contract Self-employed status Freelance

ACTIVITY 11

1   Think about past experiences in any work situation, including Saturday or holiday jobs, unpaid work experience or voluntary work. If you have never had any jobs, think of things you have enjoyed or disliked about your leisure time in terms of travel, people, hours, environment etc.

2   Make a list of any working conditions that have turned out to be particularly important to you or that you believe will be important in future life.

3   When you analyse job vacancies look for clues related to these various aspects.

SUMMARY

1   Self-awareness helps you make the most of your strengths and choose appropriate types of work.

2   The best way to identify skills and interests is to look back over your life and discover what you did well and enjoyed.

2   The principles we live by often come into evidence when conflicts arise at work, and being aware of your values and needs will help you choose whether to stay in a job or not.

4   People often describe their job in terms of the working conditions, and these can have a strong influence on enjoyment or satisfaction at work.

5   By collecting together the results of all the activities in this Step, you will have built up an honest and full picture of yourself that you can use when job-hunting.

DECIDING WHAT TO DO

There are various theories related to career decision-making, and the most common scenario is one that views it as a three-stage process:

Stage one – identify what you are good at, what you enjoy and what your values and needs might be.

Stage two – find out as much as possible about the world of work, what types of employment are available and what work roles they offer.

Stage three – match the profile you create after carrying out your self-analysis to various job profiles and narrow down your choice to a few career options.

STEERING VERSUS PLANNING

It is a very strange idea that for those of you aged just twenty-one or so, perhaps with little or no work experience and after spending most of your time in full-time education, any of you can know what you want to do for the next ten or twenty years of your lives. Yet somehow it has become expected that you are not only ready to apply for jobs during your final year but will be able to justify your choice. If you were on a vocational degree course, you may even have made your career decision as early as your mid-teens.

This book is about being realistic, and so although some of you may be able to decide early and plan your career path, it is quite likely that many more of you will actually spend the next few years zigzagging through a variety of jobs, steering your way through life as you earn. Fortunately, at each point of change, you will know a little more about yourself and what type of work you want to do or would enjoy and can take more control over the path you follow. You may also find that, as you build up your network of contacts or work with different people in various organizations, opportunities can arise out of the blue.

EXAMPLE

A 2012 psychology graduate didn't know what she wanted to do but, walking down the high street, saw a card in the window of a clothes shop offering a part-time sales assistant job. After a few months, she decided she needed to work more hours and so took another part-time sales job with a chemist. Eventually, she was offered full-time work at the chemist. A few months later, she was offered training as a pharmacy dispenser which, having watched and talked to staff in that area, she thought she would enjoy.

As pharmacies are found in supermarkets and the NHS as well as chemist shops, she now has a wide range of opportunities for developing a supervisory and then managerial career in any of these businesses. Without a pharmacy degree, she would eventually have to move into the main business, but could specialize in one of a variety of areas, including staff training, human resources, customer service or line management.

Often, careers are only visible by looking backwards. It is amazing how, even though at the time you may feel your various jobs are unrelated, a pattern emerges and you find you have steered yourself towards sensible and constructive choices that build up a solid picture of a 'career' or even two or three careers.

EXAMPLE

Looking back over my own career, I find these basic elements:

1   Science degree
2   Temping as a secretary
3   Working overseas as a secretary
4   Secretarial work, including committee work
5   Admin/committee work in a business confederation's education and training department
6   PR/committee work in an engineering institution
7   University careers work, initially in a science/engineering institution
8   PGCE – teacher training
9   Running a CV design service using my careers experience
10 Teaching adults English, maths and computing
11 Adult IT tutor and trainer
12 Writing IT books
13 Writing other books
14 Writing tutor

Links in the chain are: science – secretary – committee work – education and training – careers work – teaching – computing – writing.

Postgraduate education or training

The one area where you will need to be more of a planner than a navigator, making early decisions about your career, is if you are considering taking further qualifications. As this is quite a commitment, both financially and in terms of time, it is not a decision to be taken lightly. But there are certain circumstances where it may be unavoidable if you want to go down a particular career path or work in certain areas, at least for the next few years.

43

ACTIVITY 12

1   Are you considering further study?

2   What is your main reason?

The most common reasons for further study include:

- Aiming for an academic career. Most lectureships or university research posts are so competitive that it is very unlikely that a graduate with just a first degree will be offered a position.

- Knowing you want to join a profession such as teaching, counselling or law, or even medicine or psychology that are also open to later-entrant graduates from all disciplines, will require a postgraduate certificate, diploma or other conversion course qualification if your first degree is unrelated.

- For many careers, including those such as journalism, museum and gallery work, film-making, acting etc., which are highly competitive, or where others may already have a relevant degree or years of work experience, it may be your best chance of securing a job – especially if the course includes some form of work placement.

- Feeling you need further skills or a specialism, to build up a portfolio of work or even to make the contacts or have the kudos of studying at a prestigious UK or international institution (such as one of the famous music, art or fashion colleges). In such cases it can be worthwhile spending one or more years studying further.

- Completely changing direction. If you have none of the relevant skills or experience, it may be the only alternative to an apprenticeship or on-the-job training.

Note that most people would advise you to get relevant work experience rather than 'waste money' on a postgraduate course that is simply helping you further towards a competitive career, but like the chicken and the egg, which comes first? Ideally, apply for the course and at the same time apply for a direct-entry job or training position, or even take any job you can find to fund voluntary or work experience in your chosen field. If the right job comes first, you can then cancel your place.

Perhaps the most caution should be exercised if you are considering an MA or equivalent (especially if it is just because you don't know what you want to do). If it follows on from your degree course and you are not taking it as a conversion course or prequel to studying for a doctorate, this will simply take your degree discipline one year further on. For anyone who knows they may soon want to leave their subject behind, it could really be a wasted year.

ACTIVITY 13

1 Are you fairly sure about the type of work you want to do, the skills you want to use and/or the work environment you would enjoy? For example, do you know you want to work with books (e.g. in libraries or publishing), help the vulnerable (e.g. in counselling or social care) or go into finance (e.g. investment banking or accountancy)?

2 If the answer is yes, you may be ready to explore the world of work in Step 3

3 If the answer is no, read on and carry out the next Activity.

PROBLEMS WITH MATCHING

Sometimes the three-stage planning approach works out. Here are two examples of using the process outlined earlier:

1 If you are good at and enjoy sport (stage one), you might want to start by exploring the various careers involved with sport such

as athlete, commentating, coaching, umpiring, leisure-centre management, sports writing, PE teaching or sports photography (stage two). By analysing each type of job in turn, you might end up seriously considering two or three where you can also use your skills in instructing or writing (stage three).

2 If you are interested in films (stage one), you may decide to find out more about editing, directing, production, screen or scriptwriting, special effects, financing, film history, photography, animation, agents, cinema management or set design (stage two). Again, looking into the various careers in depth, you may focus on film work that also involves your enthusiasm for IT or design (stage three).

ACTIVITY 14

See if the process will work for you:

1 Write down three interests/skills you think you might like to use in a job. Use a separate piece of paper for each suggestion.

2 Jot down as many ideas for possible job types or relevant employers that come into your head for each one, just as in the above examples.

3 Narrow these down to three or four serious possibilities and keep them in mind as you work through the book.

Although this sounds very simple and straightforward, it can be hard in many cases to carry out this process in isolation, and even more so if you have not had years of previous work experience. Human beings are both skilled at and interested in a large number of different things, so how do you narrow down your choice to just a few? For example, what do you do if you enjoy sport and film equally – apart from make a sequel to *Chariots of Fire*?

Drawbacks of concentrating on one key skill

Let us imagine that you like the idea of a job that involves writing. According to the lists of jobs available on various careers websites, there are a large number of jobs that require employees to be able to write (see just ten random job types listed below). As very few jobs involve writing alone, you would need far more detail about the work before it would help you decide if you wanted to take on a job involving:

➢ Writing detailed reports and making presentations as an actuary

➢ Writing newsletters, brochures and press releases as a public relations officer

➢ Writing stories and bulletins ready for presentation as a broadcast journalist

➢ Writing, or helping clients to write, career action plans as a careers adviser

➢ Keeping records of patients and writing reports as a dietician

➢ Writing tender submissions to raise finance as a bid writer

➢ Preparing written descriptions to give to potential buyers as an estate agent

➢ Compiling family histories for clients as a genealogist

➢ Writing advertising or marketing material as a copywriter

➢ Writing up exercise programmes as a personal trainer

One of the important factors would be how much writing is actually involved in any of these roles. If you want the majority of your time to be spent writing, many of the above jobs would probably not appeal. But concentrating on writing jobs alone would leave out too many other possibilities, and ignoring jobs that don't involve one particular key skill or interest could do you a great disservice.

The problem with making too much of strengths and interests is that you may get great satisfaction from a job that doesn't feature one specific ability or interest such as writing, sport or film. If you do discover jobs you would like to do that don't happen to make use of a particular skill/interest, you have three choices: put that subject aside altogether; keep it as a hobby; or try to build it into your work at some time in the future.

In other words, you may find a perfectly suitable job despite having a strong interest or ability in something unrelated to it.

Using skills

Another aspect of skills is that it is often hard to know if you do have the skill, what level you have reached or whether and how you might want to use it. For example, what interpersonal skills do you have? Here is just a sample of the various ways this skill might be applied:

➢ One-to-one (e.g. counselling)

➢ With small groups (e.g. running focus groups)

➢ With large audiences (e.g. lecturing)

➢ Serving customers (e.g. retail sales)

➢ Taking instructions (e.g. trainee pilot)

➢ Disciplining (e.g. human resources manager)

➢ Educating/teaching/training (e.g. driving instructor)

➢ Guiding a discussion (e.g. tutoring)

➢ Facilitating (e.g. running workshops)

➢ Persuading (e.g. campaign manager)

➢ Motivating (e.g. football manager)

➢ Entertaining (e.g. performance poet)

➢ Analysing (e.g. product designer)

➢ Diagnosing (e.g. IT help desk support)

➢ Soothing (e.g. nursery nurse)

➤ Presenting (e.g. statistician)

➤ Imparting information (e.g. museum guide)

➤ Advising (e.g. housing officer)

➤ Coaching (e.g. badminton instructor)

➤ Counselling (e.g. drugs adviser)

➤ Listening (e.g. doctor)

Out of context, it is hard to make any decisions about which jobs you should target that would make use of this diverse skill.

Job profiles

Just as difficult as creating a meaningful personal profile is finding detailed enough job profiles for matching purposes. That is because they can only be a very superficial picture of the particular type of work and are usually less about the required personal qualities, skills and interests and more about the aims of the organization or the general work tasks. Two different people can take the same job and carry it out in completely different ways.

If we look at the example of primary school teaching, here is one job profile provided by the graduate careers website www.prospects. ac.uk:

Primary school teachers develop schemes of work and lesson plans in line with curriculum objectives. They facilitate learning by establishing a relationship with pupils and by their organization of learning resources and the classroom learning environment. Primary school teachers develop and foster the appropriate skills and social abilities to enable the optimum development of children, according to age, ability and aptitude. They assess and record progress and prepare pupils for examinations.

Four different people could be equally happy and successful primary school teachers as Teacher A may get the most satisfaction out of planning, organizing and assignment setting; Teacher B may concentrate more on the pupil contact, supported learning and organizing after-school activities; Teacher C may prefer being involved in the administration, meetings or development of technological teaching aids; and Teacher D may be particularly interested in becoming a specialist in their degree subject.

To confirm this, all you have to do is think back to your own primary school days and you will probably remember a number of very different characters, who all brought something unique to their classrooms.

Can one personality or skill set fit all?

The idea that one job type (such as primary school teacher, journalist, IT consultant or forensic scientist) requires one personality type or certain set of capabilities and interests is obviously quite ridiculous, and yet matching depends on making this assumption.

If we take the role of a sales assistant or shop owner, just imagine yourself working in a shop or at a counter selling:

- Children's books
- Mobile phones
- Specialist cheeses, tea or coffee
- Dress fabrics
- Antiques
- General groceries
- Items worth £1
- Cosmetics
- Computer repair services

It is obvious that, in many cases the vital part of the job will involve discussing and advising customers about their specialist requirements: which books a parent might buy for their five-year-old; what software they might need for a particular computing task; the right colour lipstick for their skin colouring; or which wine goes with gorgonzola. Talking to parents, computer owners, the fashion-conscious or dinner-party hosts will require varied interests and skills.

In some areas, like mobile-phone sales, persuasive skills are likely to be the most relevant as, once staff are familiar with the details of the different packages, it is signatures and contracts that are far more important than building a rapport with customers.

The approach would be quite different again in a £1 store or supermarket where knowing where items are on the shelves, managing the queues and being able to check out goods quickly and efficiently are often the most vital tasks.

EXAMPLE

In case you are wondering why sales assistant work features in a graduate job-hunting book, don't forget that in most retail careers, shop floor experience is seen as extremely relevant and valuable. It has been the starting point for many, including Alex Gourlay, Chief Executive at Boots, and Mark Harrison, Group Retail Director at Morrisons, who reached the highest levels in retail management. If you missed out on a retail graduate training scheme position this year, shop floor experience will certainly help you if you plan to apply again in the future. It is also one of the easier jobs for graduates to obtain as a first job in order to gain work experience and transferable skills.

To confirm the fact that sales jobs may not be so unusual for graduates in 2014, an article in the *Guardian*, published in 2012, stated that: 'Researchers warned that highly qualified young people were routinely being expected to take on "low-skilled" roles to fill gaps in the workforce. It emerged that the number of ex-students in "non-graduate" jobs such as office juniors or shelf stackers has soared by almost 3,500 – six per cent – this year compared with 2011.' What they should have gone on to say is that, having started at a low base, graduates are more likely to build on that experience to make positive career choices later.

To show how difficult the matching process can be, here are thirteen capabilities or interests that could be used at work:

➤ Writing	➤ Planning and organizing
➤ Communicating verbally	➤ Computing
➤ Negotiating and persuading	➤ Creativity
➤ Cooperating	➤ Languages
➤ Investigating or analysing	➤ Practical
➤ Leading	➤ Scientific or technical
➤ Numeracy	

Having identified your key capabilities or interests, you may be told that certain jobs are especially relevant. But if you were thinking of teaching, for example, it would be hard not to conclude that you would need most of these. And what skills or interests on the list wouldn't an estate agent or police officer, computer help desk assistant or clinical trials administrator need?

When you find information on types of work, they often suggest that you will need a particular subset of skills and interests, but be careful about relying too heavily on these to narrow down your choice. For example, here are the suggested qualities needed by librarians taken from three different careers information sources:

List 1

➤ Good information and communication technology (ICT) skills
➤ Good general knowledge or knowledge within a specialized field
➤ Natural curiosity
➤ Organizational and managerial skills
➤ Communication skills and confidence
➤ The ability to skim-read large amounts of text
➤ To be approachable

List 2

- ICT
- Teaching
- Enquiry
- Cataloguing
- Database use
- Foreign languages
- Communication
- Customer service
- Marketing
- Enthusiasm
- Teamwork
- Can work under pressure

List 3

- Knowledge and a passion for all things literary
- To be a perfectionist, be committed and completely meticulous
- Highly organized
- Good IT skills and willingness to keep up to date
- Customer orientated

Not only are most of the capabilities, such as IT literate, enthusiastic, enquiring, customer orientated, can work under pressure, teamwork etc., appropriate for the majority of jobs nowadays, they are also far too vague to be easily matched to any specific work roles.

On the other hand, when you view details of the various activities you might be asked to perform taken from a number of lengthy job descriptions and, even better, an actual job advertisement, these include:

- Attractive presentation of stock
- Ensure that premises remain safe and in a good state of repair
- Promote awareness of electronic services and assist customers in their use
- Serve customers
- Join new members
- Shelve returned items

From this, you get a reasonably good idea of the work and can analyse it in terms of your own interests and skills. You will also see that, for example, using foreign languages, being able to skim-read and being highly organized may not actually be required for this post even though it was suggested in the job profiles that they were key skills. Believing that they were required for all library posts could well have put you off considering the career as a whole.

Making the job fit

What usually happens when anyone takes a job is that they mould it as far as they can to fit their personal interests, needs and capabilities. This could mean that you:

- Plan and follow the process of self-analysis and job profiling, identifying careers that would make use of your key interests and abilities and applying for work in those areas

- Navigate from job to job by applying for a series of positions that you feel you could carry out and would enjoy

Once in a post you can now work at making the job fit your personal requirements as closely as possible or steer your own career path through the organization.

Career choice cannot be a simple matching process of self and job profiles because it often needs other ingredients. One such ingredient is information about the working conditions (such as hours, location, pay etc.) and another is an in-depth job description. It is only when you analyse a real job in great detail that you start to see exactly what would be involved and can decide if, taken together, the various elements add up to a job you want and can do.

Perhaps the best approach is to do both things simultaneously: identify your personal qualities and come up with ideas for types of work that complement your strengths and interests and, at the same time, explore a wide range of actual vacancies or types of work. Select any that seem to offer the most in terms of suiting your personal requirements and hope they are flexible enough for you to add your own emphasis once in post.

FANTASY JOBS

Do you have a fantasy or dream job? There are certain jobs that some people, whatever their background or educational level, aspire to, because they offer what appear to be easy routes to fame, money, power or status. These include:

- ➢ Professional sportsman
- ➢ Astronaut
- ➢ Top businesswoman
- ➢ Novelist

- ➢ Senior politician
- ➢ Rock star
- ➢ TV personality
- ➢ Stand-up comic

If you are particularly keen on any of these, or similarly hard-to-get jobs, they are still achievable but will require some or all of the following:

1 Real talent that is developed over a number of years through hard work and training and may still depend on a certain amount of luck if you are to be spotted.

2 Time spent building up a portfolio of work that will eventually be recognized, for example by agents, film directors or publishers.

3 Taking a series of relevant educational or training courses to acquire the necessary qualifications.

4 Taking a series of low-paid, low-level or short-term positions, 'starting at the bottom' or even volunteering to show motivation and acquire on-the-job work experience.

5 Taking risks to develop entrepreneurial skills or test the market.

6 Networking and making contacts so that you are in the best position to hear about openings and meet people with influence.

7   Being realistic – if you haven't got quite what it takes to be the very best, you can still use your talents to do something closely related. For example, if you are not good enough as a stand-up, you can still write sketches for others, or if you cannot be a rock star, you can still compose, manage a band or a studio, write music reviews, teach the guitar or be a session musician.

If your dream job seems unattainable, one way to bring it within reach is to identify the route you could take to get there and then take it one step at a time.

For example, if you want to be the next J. K. Rowling or Stephen King:

➤ Get any job you can that will provide an income – novelists often squeeze their writing into the evenings or weekends

➤ Take a writing course if you need to improve your skills

➤ Start writing anything, e.g. short stories, poems, articles and reviews and submit them to magazines and online websites, or enter writing competitions

➤ Get feedback on your writing from forums, message boards, on your own website or blog, or through fiction sites such as www.wattpad.com or www.fanfiction.net.

However difficult it will be, if you are highly motivated towards a particular career you are still luckier than most, because you have a goal and can at least identify the steps you need to take to achieve it. For most people, knowing which direction to go in can be the hardest thing to identify.

ACTIVITY 15

1 If you could do any job at all, what would it be?

2 Identify five different reasons for your choice.

3 Is there a pattern, e.g. does it require the same skills or satisfy the same needs as other work you have considered, or is it unique?

4 Could you identify a step-by-step approach to achieving your goal?

ROUTES INTO WORK

In the real world, there are many different ways in which you could end up applying for jobs. In the main, universities are best at helping highly motivated graduates follow a straightforward route – either towards further education or to find a specific graduate-entry position through the Milkround, job fairs or by using the careers service contact lists.

But here are seven quite different routes you could take:

Route 1: A friend or family member hears about a job, perhaps at their own place of work, and suggests you apply.

Route 2: You approach organizations based locally and they offer you an interview for a job that you may know little about.

Route 3: You register with recruitment agencies and look through the local paper, online vacancies or on the student union jobs pages and apply for anything that looks possible.

Route 4: You see a card in a shop window that may have very few details on it and phone up about the job.

Route 5: You contact organizations in the appropriate field, following an enjoyable holiday job or leisure activity to see if they have any vacancies.

Route 6: You follow up a list of employers who employ people with your degree discipline.

Route 7: You obtain a role inside an organization, perhaps as a temporary worker or volunteer, and look out for vacancies from within.

Applying self-awareness

Without realizing it, you will be using your self-awareness to make decisions about who to contact or which jobs to target. For example:

- **Job 1** (word of mouth) – if you are told there are vacancies in finance, reception and sales – one of these is likely to appeal more than others. Why?

- **Job 2** (local businesses) – hundreds of organizations will be based locally, so which ten or so have you targeted, and why a local company and not a national one?

- **Job 3** (vacancy lists) – local papers, employment agencies and websites have thousands of jobs on offer, so what are the criteria you are using to narrow these down?

- **Job 4** (shop windows) – cards in windows usually offer a wide range of part-time and self-employment positions, so why do certain ones appeal most?

- **Job 5** (following up an interest) – if following up a hobby or previous work experience, what have you enjoyed about the activity that makes you want to carry on with it as a career?

- **Job 6** (using your degree) – in what way do you want to use your subject, considering the number of different opportunities there are likely to be for graduates with your qualifications?

▪ **Job 7** (discovering from within) – what has made you pick that particular organization to work for, and what makes you decide which internal vacancies to apply for or the departments to approach?

As you can see, the more you understand your own motivation, the easier and more logical the choices will be.

SUMMARY

1   Some people can plan their careers in advance by matching their personal profile with job details, whereas others may be better suited to steering a course through life as they move on from one job to the next.

2   To go on to further study, you need to know exactly why you are doing it, as it is quite a financial as well as a time commitment.

3   Just because you have a particular skill or interest doesn't mean you should only look at jobs that will make the most use of it.

4   No one personality or skill set is required for particular types of work as different people can carry out the same work by moulding the job to suit their requirements.

5   There are a number of different routes into work and any one could turn out to be successful.

STEP 3

FINDING OUT ABOUT WORK

Having identified your strengths and preferences you should now be able to make a little more sense of the world of work. Hopefully this self-awareness will help you identify certain areas of work on which to concentrate your efforts or those that you should definitely avoid.

This chapter is about employment, but even if you want to run your own business it is still necessary to see what opportunities may be out there and where you might fit in. Also, for anyone hoping to work as a self-employed or freelance consultant or specialist, you often need to have several years' experience working for others first.

WHERE THE JOBS ARE

If you spent just ten minutes brainstorming, you would probably be able to come up with a hundred job titles, based on your experience at school, university, in your family, through leisure pursuits, or even just out shopping and travelling. That is because there are thousands of different types of work available and exploring what you could do or would enjoy can be a time-consuming business.

Perhaps the easiest way to cope is to narrow down your search to particular groups of jobs that have something in common. Here are five different approaches:

- By employment sector – organizations can be grouped into twenty or so different sectors related to their products or services

- By work activities – many jobs will be carried out across a variety of different sectors and it may be more helpful to concentrate first on the tasks before identifying where you could carry them out

■ By overall aims or personal preferences – create your own personal list of employment areas based on your priorities

■ By degree or subject relevance, if you want to make the most of your university studies

■ Locally – finding out about small enterprises, hubs, research parks and other potential employers based in your area

Working overseas

Don't forget that you can do the same jobs overseas, but it will obviously be harder to find out about opportunities and apply than if the employers are in the UK. As well as getting advice from your careers service, two websites offering advice and details of graduate employment overseas are STA Travel and Euro Graduate.

Employment sectors

When you put the words 'employment sectors' or 'job sectors' into any search engine, you will be offered around a score or so of broad categories. Although the classifications can vary, most lists will usually include:

Health and social care	Media and publishing
Education and training	Advertising, marketing and PR
Finance	Hospitality and tourism
Law	Property and construction
Retail and sales	Arts and heritage
Public sector	Agriculture and environment
Engineering and manufacturing	Armed forces and emergency
Science and pharmaceuticals	services

Many companies or individuals could belong to one of several sectors (for example, is an educational or scientific publisher within the education, science or publishing sector, and is a dispensing optician in the health or sales sector?) so it should be seen only as an overview, but one that can be a useful starting point if you are strongly attracted to a particular activity, product or service.

- If you explore some of the employment sectors in more depth, you may be able to identify different avenues to follow. For example:

- Health and social care covers both public and private dental practices, medical practices, hospitals, nursing homes and day centres, (and it might logically include social services departments normally classified under the public sector).

- Science and pharmaceuticals includes laboratory R and D, chemical, oil, gas, polymer, nuclear and pharmaceutical industries, scientific publishing, patents and technology transfer.

- Armed forces and emergency services includes the police, fire, ambulance, Army, Navy and Air Force together with private companies supplying catering, medical services, vehicles, weapons and surveillance equipment.

If the idea of working in any of these areas appeals, you can find out about types of work specific to each sector. For example, specialist health and social care jobs include:

Acupuncturist	Osteopath
Nurse	Dietician
Radiologist	Art/Music/Drama therapist
Occupational therapist	Clinical psychologist
Counsellor	Paramedic
Doctor	Home visitor
Dentist	Midwife
Chiropractor	Social worker

And some of the specialist posts in the public sector include:

Advice worker

Civil Service administrator

Community education officer

Counsellor

Government social research officer

Immigration officer

Intelligence analyst/officer

Local government officer

Politician's assistant

Probation officer

Social worker

Trading standards officer

Waste management officer

The graduate careers website www.prospects.ac.uk provides resources to help you work through job sectors to identify many of the specialist jobs you could do, and to find out more about types of work, entry requirements and employment opportunities. Although it concentrates on graduate employment, you should get a good idea of the environment in which you would be working even if you start in a non-graduate position.

ACTIVITY 16

1 Look through the employment sectors listed above and select three that appeal most.

2 Select the three that appeal least.

3 What are your main reasons for each choice?

Work activities

If you don't want to train for any of the specialist posts, there are still a huge number of other jobs available within each sector, and many of these are found across a wide range of completely different organizations. So it may be more helpful to identify suitable tasks and activities before deciding where you might work.

For example, if you like the idea of teaching, there are posts for:

➤ Teachers in schools

➢ Lecturers in universities and colleges

➢ Tutors in the community

➢ Driving instructors in private firms

➢ Sports coaches with clubs or employed by local authorities

➢ Music, art, craft or exam preparation private tutors

➢ Instructors with the armed forces

➢ Teaching english as a foreign language in private colleges

➢ Trainers of new equipment or software in companies

➢ Staff and management trainers in both the public and private sector

Administrators can work in theatres, galleries, schools, local government, the Civil Service, police forces, industrial company offices, law firms, universities, hospitals and clinics.

Cooks are employed in staff canteens, schools, hospitals, airports and airlines, in developing supermarket products, as private caters, in restaurants, pubs and cafés and as cookery writers.

If you would like to explore some of the hundreds of job types available, it is probably easiest to start online at one of the careers or recruitment agency websites where you will find alphabetical lists of jobs together with their job descriptions. These will list many of the activities you would be expected to perform. By keeping in mind your personal profile and the need to look at real adverts as well as generalized job descriptions, it should not take too long to run your eye down the list and pick out any job types you feel might be worth exploring. It is also an excellent way to familiarize yourself with jobs you know little about. Two useful websites are www.prospects.ac.uk/ types_of_jobs_browse_all.htm and targetjobs.co.uk/careers-advice/ job-descriptions (over three hundred listed).

To give you an idea of the range, here are ten random examples:

➢ Court reporter   ➢ Packaging technologist

➢ Housing adviser   ➢ Personal assistant

➢ Features editor   ➢ Project manager

➢ Media planner   ➢ Recycling officer

➢ Nature conservation officer   ➢ Youth worker

ACTIVITY 17

1   To test your knowledge of job types, do you know what people in each of the above jobs would do?

2   If you had to choose one job from the list, which would it be and why?

3   Which would be your least favourite, and why?

There are two further valuable sources of information about types of work:

▪ Professional bodies are set up to provide information and support to members as well as oversee professional qualifications. If you think you might want to be anything from a librarian to an accountant, archivist, lawyer, biochemist or copywriter, there will probably be an institute, association or society relevant to you. To find one, type 'professional body – (job type)' into a search engine and relevant organizations should be listed.

▪ Ask people who do the job to tell you about it. It can be extremely helpful to find out what they like and dislike about their work, what made them apply, what their prospects might be and how they got in. It could save you many hours if it turns out that what they say puts you off or they suggest a completely different route to take.

Personal priorities

Using your own personal criteria, it is possible to devise a hierarchy of jobs based on particular aims or related to specific working conditions. These will cut across different classifications such as employment sector or general work activity and may also be duplicated depending on the criteria. For example:

- **Working outdoors** – this could include farming and agriculture, rural crafts, fisheries, shipping, construction, working with animals, campsite management, events organization, rangers, groundskeeper, forestry, sports or coaching

- **Helping others** – this may relate to jobs in social care, education, health, local government, emergency services, charities, international organizations

- **Related to the environment** – jobs with this aim can be in research, manufacturing, education, journalism, politics, planning, agriculture, forestry, water or waste management

- **Creative jobs** – not only those in radio, film, TV, performing arts, design and photography, but also in publishing, journalism, advertising, architecture, manufacturing and construction

If you prefer to start exploring types of work under these sorts of headings, as well as carrying out a general 'outdoors jobs' or 'caring jobs' type internet search, you can visit careers websites such as Kent University's Careers Service: www.kent.ac.uk/careers/workin.htm. Here their indexes list jobs under the heading 'I want to work in . . .' and feature 'with children', 'outdoor and active', 'helping careers' etc. as well as the more conventional classifications.

You could also type your keywords like 'outdoors' or 'environment' into the 'What is Your Dream Job?' search box at nationalcareersservice.direct.gov.uk or take a light-hearted look at jobs for sporty, creative, practical, outgoing, foodie, geek or academic etc. people at www.totaljobs.com/careers-advice/what-job-can-i-do.

ACTIVITY 18

1 Can you complete this sentence: 'I would like a job that involves . . .'

2 If you have written something down, come up with at least three different jobs that would be appropriate.

Work related to your degree

Most university departments and careers offices will have information on where past graduates have gone and the employers and jobs relevant to your degree.

Some degrees don't seem to lead to anything specifically except teaching, researching or writing about the subject, but in other cases there will usually be a number of jobs available that either only graduates from your discipline can do or where your degree is particularly welcomed or preferred. You should be able to find information on both graduate-level jobs and related technical or assistant posts that might be a more achievable starting point.

If we take history, www.kent.ac.uk/careers/history.htm lists four further occupations closely related to the subject: archaeologist, archivist, tour guide and museum curator, and many more occupations where the degree would be useful.

For drama, they suggest relevant careers include actor, stage manager, arts administrator, drama therapist and TV or radio presenter.

As with types of work, there are many societies, associations and institutions relevant to different degree subjects, including the Institute of Physics, the Royal Society of Chemistry and the European Association of Archaeologists. To use their resources, try locating the bodies with a general Web search or visit www.totalprofessions.com/profession-finder. If you type your degree subject into the search box or use the subject index, relevant bodies will be listed that you can then follow up.

Local enterprises

Wherever you live, a town near you may well have a thriving business sector that is little known about or advertised but which can offer employment opportunities. One of the best ways to learn about these is to read the local business press – newspapers, newsletters and magazines; they are always trying to promote local success stories. Another is through umbrella organizations or federations such as the Local Enterprise Partnerships, Chambers of Commerce or Federation of Small Businesses. Physically, you could go round your local university or other science parks, business parks or creative hubs, noting the names of companies and calling in to pick up brochures or find out what they do. There may also be networking clubs, exhibitions or other events you could attend.

Here are just a few local examples to show you where you could go for further information – other regions of the country are likely to have similar bodies or groups:

➢ Hereford and Worcester Chamber of Commerce at www. hwchamber.co.uk

➢ Federation of Small Businesses in North Wales and Cheshire at www.fsb.org.uk/northwales

➢ Bristol and Bath Science Park at www.bbsp.co.uk

➢ The Somerset House Creative Hub in London at www. somersethouse.org.uk

➢ Reading business park at www.greenpark.co.uk/property/ occupiers

Small businesses are often owned by individual entrepreneurs who are busy keeping the company going, and as they employ few people you need to take a direct and targeted approach rather than sticking to the conventional 'letter and CV' type of job application formula.

➢ Find out as much as possible about the owner, the company and their products or services

➤ Come up with really good reasons for working for them based on what you can contribute

➤ Find one or two skills you can offer that will be immediately helpful – they may not have time for long-term training

➤ Be proactive – arrange to have a chat with someone to put forward your case for employment

FURTHER QUALIFICATIONS

To progress in many careers, and especially if you are changing direction from your original degree subject, you are quite likely to need further qualifications and training. There are a variety of ways in which these can be achieved, including:

➤ Full-time study in a college or university

➤ Part-time study at college or via distance learning or online courses

➤ In-house or other training offered by your employer

➤ Self-study using books, distance learning or online materials

➤ Apprenticeships, where you are paid a lower wage but receive both training and work experience

Costs may be met by your employer or you may have to pay for yourself, apply for a grant or take out a loan. It is worth taking great care before launching into expensive, long-term training, as it may be possible to get a job that provides just as relevant experience and pays at the same time. You may also find that, nowadays, part-time courses are a less expensive but perfectly acceptable route. Although there are courses on every conceivable career, explore the different routes you could take very carefully before committing yourself.

SUMMARY

1 There are various ways to categorize jobs, including by sector, work type, personal preferences or related to degree subject.

2 In any sector, you could either take a specialist post or carry out work that is also available across a wide range of different organizations.

3 Small companies based locally often need to be approached differently as you may have to persuade them to take a graduate on.

4 If you require further qualifications, check out the various routes to find the most cost-effective.

STEP 4

GETTING READY TO APPLY

Applying for jobs usually means convincing an employer that they should interview you, not that they should give you the job. Once you are face-to-face or talking over the telephone, a whole new set of criteria will come into play. So what can you do to make sure you move on to the interview stage?

WHAT EMPLOYERS WANT

If you imagine an employer faced with hundreds of applications for a single post, it is fairly clear that the main aims will be to:

➤ Reject unsuitable candidates as quickly as possible

➤ Identify candidates who seem to have most of what they want

➤ Reduce this number down to a manageable size

Rejections

Large organizations may employ a range of staff to sift through and reject as many applications as possible by following laid-down criteria, or it may be the task of human resources staff or senior managers. With computerized applications increasing all the time, built-in filters will be applied but they will all be looking for similar things:

1 **Do you meet the basic criteria?** If, for example, they require GCSEs in maths and English, or an engineering degree,

applications without these qualifications will probably not progress further (unless, for example, you have discussed any non-standard qualifications with them in advance).

2 **Have you followed the rules?** For paper applications, if they ask for an application form but get a CV or just a letter, you will normally be rejected immediately.

3 **Is the application well presented?** If they are looking for reasons to reject people, sending in scruffy, hard-to-read documentation, or too much information, is a good start.

4 **Are there gaps?** If any sections are empty, particularly the 'why do you want to work for us?' type open-ended question boxes, the application will be rejected.

To avoid rejection, the rules are clear:

➢ Follow the instructions exactly

➢ Complete every section

➢ Make sure you meet all the basic criteria

➢ Present your application as attractively as possible

What employers are looking for

If we assume your application is now in the 'to be considered' category, employers are going to be looking for evidence of the following:

1 You can do the work and have the right attitude, i.e. you have the relevant skills, experience, personal qualities, specific transferable skills, physical traits and special requirements, such as a driving licence or your own transport etc., if asked for. In some cases, they may also need to make sure you can be trained in areas where you do not yet have the relevant skills. Most graduates should, by default, meet that criterion.

2 You are motivated to work for them – you want the job, want

to work in their organization and want what they are offering now and in the future. This is not the same as applying for a job that meets your personal needs of money, security, status etc. You need to show that you can make a clear connection between who you are and what you can bring to the organization.

3   You would fit in, i.e. would get on with colleagues/customers and would have the appropriate values.

4   That you have the more general transferable skills (see list on page 16) that seem to be demanded for most jobs.

They will also be checking:

➢ That you do not have any undesirable qualities or attitudes

➢ To see if you have something special about you

➢ That you have the potential to go far in their organization without being motivated unrealistically – for example, not wanting something they cannot offer

ACTIVITY 19

1   Over the next pages you will find four different advertisements for jobs.

2   For each one, try to identify what you would have to offer to meet the major requirements set out above.

3   Then read the analysis below.

1   **Can you do the work?**
You will see that, in most of these examples, it is very hard to pinpoint exactly what employers want as they talk in vague terms about personal qualities and the ideal mix of transferable skills rather than what you would actually do, from which you could glean the relevant skills or experiences you might need. You have to read between the lines if necessary and come up with examples of experience that relates to what they are looking for

- **Classified sales** – ability to build a rapport with people, manage a client base, generate advertising revenue, target new clients, highly focused, practical, use your initiative, solve problems quickly, ambitious, self-starter, positive, tenacious, enthusiastic, persistent, patient and flexible, outgoing and fun-loving, drive and determination

  - Have you ever sold anything, have telephone expertise or initiated/started something and can you provide evidence of drive, ambition, tenacity and good communication skills?

- **Teaching assistant** – help a child with Asperger's syndrome in class, set assignments, relate to parents and staff, give feedback, understand the child's ability and progress made

  - Have you ever worked in a school, worked or spent time with children, helped someone with homework, related to managers, written reports or given feedback? Do you understand the education system or how people learn, have knowledge of Asperger's syndrome or other disabilities?

- **Librarian** – manage and deliver an enquiry service, present stock, ensure premises remain safe and in a good state of repair, report faults and risks, line manage staff, act as Duty Officer for Borough Libraries, serve customers, join new members, shelve returned items, assist customers with enquiries, promote awareness of electronic services and assist customers in their use, housekeeping and administrative duties, flexible and with physical stamina

  - Have you ever worked in a library, helped anyone with computer problems, managed staff, worked with customers? Can you show a love of books and reading, and that you have stamina?

- **Telefónica graduate scheme** – no tasks mentioned, just requirements such as minimum 2:1 degree, fluent English and additional language skills a plus (German, Slovak, Czech or Spanish), strong commercial awareness, analytical skills, relationship management and communication skills, effective decision making, online IT / digital skills

- Do you have experience of O2, the telecommunications industry, working or living abroad, analysing, making decisions? Do you understand commerce and have good online IT or digital skills?
- They may look for motivation and the ability to learn languages if you have none.

2 **Would you want the job?**
You need to show that you would enjoy working in the place, organization, situation or role specified.

- **Classified sales** – you would need to like the media and consumer magazines and be happy to work in London in what appears to be a highly pressurized sales environment

- **Teaching assistant** – happy to work in a school, in Redbridge, one-to-one with a disabled child, would enjoy relating to parents and staff, be willing to undergo CRB checks

- **Librarian** – happy to work on Sundays, in Maidenhead, in a library, dealing with the public and routine tasks, using computers, willing to undergo CRB checks, can accept the short hours and fixed contract

- **Telefónica graduate scheme** – interested in telecommunications, want to work in departments such as Marketing, IT and Networks, Leadership and European Leadership, willing to live in Slough, happy to be on a two-year training programme. Any indication that you don't want to travel or be away from home would be unwelcome

3 **Would you fit in?**
This is where they will be looking for an obvious mismatch between you and perhaps the age of the people you will be working with; your attitudes to the environment or tasks; and any other aspects where you seem to indicate you would not enjoy or would be unable to cope with things asked of you.

- **Classified sales** – if they know that most of their staff are young, sociable, ambitious, with lots of drive and all your interests are lone pursuits or you are older than thirty-five, they will want to see evidence that any assumptions about you are wrong

- **Teaching assistant** – as this is a responsible and sensitive job, any sign that you are immature, inexperienced or might not be able to speak up would be of concern

- **Librarian** – again, having to help customers of all ages and come in on Sundays might mean they would prefer a mature, reliable person and would want to see evidence of that in your application

- **Telefónica graduate scheme** – they may expect applicants to be young, adventurous risk-takers who are happy to mix with other young people as well as be trained by youngish managers. If you are far older or have established a base in the UK, you may need to show you get on well with young people and are willing to travel

Advert 1

CLASSIFIED SALES EXECUTIVE
Consumer Magazine
London – £18,000–£20,000 + commission

My client is looking for a motivated, ambitious individual who wants to build a career within media sales. Working for this well-known consumer magazine, the right candidate will be hard-working and tenacious, with an ability to build rapport with people. This role focuses on building client relationships and generating advertising revenue.

Key Responsibilities:
In the role as a Classified Sales Executive you will be expected to:

- Manage a client base and develop relationships
- Target new clients to generate advertising revenue
- Identify new customers and build your client base

Personal Specifications

In the role as a Classified Sales Executive you will be expected to possess/be:

- An ambitious self-starter
- Positive, tenacious, enthusiastic, persistent, patient and flexible
- Passion for the media industry
- Outgoing and fun-loving

My client is looking for candidates who are highly focused, practical and who have a 'can-do' attitude and the ability to use their initiative to solve problems quickly.

Media Sales is a social environment, where building relationships with others is part of the role. For those with the drive and determination, this career can be hugely enjoyable and rewarding. If you are passionate about media, in particular magazines, then you need to apply now.

Advert 2

TEACHING ASSISTANT

Redbridge − £60−£65 per day

We are recruiting for a TA in a mainstream primary school in Redbridge, working 1:1 with a child with Asperger's syndrome. This position will be full-time Monday−Friday 8.30−4.00. Here are the responsibilities that are requested for you to take on:

- Giving the children your full attention and helping within their class
- Making sure that the child is working at their best ability
- Setting up activities and organizing ways to bring on their workload
- Developing a positive relationship with parents and staff. Giving your feedback and sharing any development
- Helping the children to work within a team and helping them get involved within class discussions

- A good understanding of the child's ability and process to work

It is essential that you hold an Enhanced CRB.

Advert 3

LIBRARIAN
Maidenhead
3–5 hours a week on Sundays at £12.38 p.h.
for a part-time,1 year fixed-term contract
CRB check: Enhanced

We are looking for an Enquiry Librarian who is enthusiastic, self-motivated and committed to excellent customer care. This is a wide-ranging role involving management and delivery of an enquiry service. Key parts of the role also include attractive presentation of stock and ensuring that premises remain safe and in a good state of repair, reporting faults and risks as they arise.

You will be required to line manage staff and to act as Duty Officer for Borough Libraries, to serve customers, join new members, shelve returned items and assist customers with enquiries. You will also be required to have sufficient skills and experience to promote awareness of electronic services and to assist customers in their use. The role includes housekeeping and administrative duties.

You will need to have good customer care skills with an interest in reading and promoting stock.

We are looking for applications from candidates who are committed to continuous improvement and lean working. A flexible approach is essential. The scope of the work is physical in nature with staff required to remain active for the duration of their shift.

You may be required to work at any location in the Borough.

Advert 4

TELEFÓNICA GRADUATE PROGRAMME
Slough – £30,000

Your adventure starts here!

We're Telefónica, a world leader in global communications and the name behind O2.

We've launched Talentum, our new approach to hiring and inspiring the brightest students and graduates across Europe. We want people who love stepping out of their comfort zones and taking on new challenges.

Here at Telefónica Europe, we're always looking for the next generation of big thinkers. People who'll push boundaries and bring bold ideas to keep our customers connecting in the years to come. So if you're ready to start your career, our Talentum programme is where your adventure begins.

So if you're a highly ambitious student our two-year graduate programme could get your career off to a flying start with positions in Marketing, IT and Networks, Leadership and European Leadership.

Requirements:

- Minimum 2:1 degree
- Fluent English + additional language skills a plus (German, Slovak, Czech or Spanish)
- Strong commercial awareness
- Analytical skills
- Relationship management and communication skills
- Effective decision-making
- Online IT/digital skills

Additional details:

- Salary information: £30,000 per annum
- Opportunities available in Slough

FINDING OUT MORE

It is very common to find that job advertisements don't tell you enough to prepare a professional application and that first, you need to find out more about the employer and the work. There are a number of sources you could go to:

- Their website – this often provides their 'mission statement' (the aims and ethos of the organization), details about their operations, their customers, their products and services, and even case studies or profiles of staff or important clients

- Follow up any offers to send you brochures and – particularly – job descriptions, and if not specified, phone up and ask if there is any background information

- Talk to people doing a similar job or within the same sector. For example, does anyone in the family work in a similar organization or role?

- Use careers service libraries or even public libraries for further information, including company or annual reports and job profiles of that type of work

- For degree-related jobs, university departmental staff may be able to help you

- Read job adverts for jobs in similar organizations as they may contain useful details

- If there is an institute or society covering this type of work, ask them for job information

- Read articles in the professional journals or newspapers for background information on the profession or sector

HIDDEN AGENDA

There are always underlying issues when it comes to employment that may not be mentioned or made explicit but need to be identified, if that is possible, before you can decide whether or not to apply for a job.

Here are a few issues you could think about:

1 **Where will I be based?** Is the office, lab, building site, garage, hospital etc. easily identifiable and acceptable? Does the location of the workplace necessitate a long, expensive journey or, perhaps, a need to travel to different places or even countries during the working day or week?

2 **Who will I be working with?** Will I be on my own most of the time, with lots of other like-minded people of my age, or with a couple of much older/younger people all day?

3 **Will I be under stress?** Is it clearly a stressful job, or will I need to be prepared to write reports, never have any privacy, have a busy schedule, have to stay up late finishing work, have to deal with difficult customers, parents, the public etc. or have to learn how to use complicated equipment very quickly?

4 **Is the job going anywhere?** A large organization with a clear management structure or which emphasizes 'promotion from within' is obviously more attractive than a one-man band with no senior positions to aim for – unless the experience is all you want.

5 **How risky is it?** This could mean physically, or financially if the contract is short-term or commission only, or for the future if the job is in a run-down area or within a threatened sector.

PROVIDING THE EVIDENCE

Once you have analysed the job in as much detail as you can, and added information from various other sources to reinforce what is in the advertisement, it is time to put together all the evidence you have that you are the right candidate. Bear in mind that you are unlikely to be able to offer everything, but as long as you can meet most requirements, you stand as good a chance as anyone else.

There are usually three main areas to cover:

➢ Skills, qualifications, experience and personal qualities

➢ Interests and attitude

➢ Working conditions

For every skill, qualification, personal quality, experience, attitude or interest mentioned, you need to ask yourself questions to help you find your evidence. For example:

1 Have I ever done that (e.g. supervised someone)?
2 Can I show that I have an interest in that (e.g. learning languages)?
3 Have I ever used that (e.g. a digital camera)?
4 Have I ever experienced that (e.g. a hospital environment)?
5 Have I ever developed that (e.g. presentation skills)?
6 Have I ever been that (e.g. a childminder)?
7 Do I have an example that shows I am that (e.g. sociable)?

If you are making a speculative application, you still need to address what they are likely to be looking for.

The evidence you cite can come from a wide range of sources, including:

1 Classes attended
2 Examinations passed
3 Certificates, awards, prizes, cups etc.
4 Working in a job or at tasks using particular skills
5 Experience from your studies, hobbies, voluntary work, leisure activities, self-directed learning etc.
6 Life in general – responsibilities, relationships and experiences

Essential and desirable

Looking at any job advertisement, it is important not to be put off if you do not have all the Desirable qualities, but you do need to have the Essential qualities. Before you start you should also look up any terms or jargon you don't understand, rather than ignore them or leave them out of your application.

On page 85 is an example of part of a job description for a Graduate Publishing Editor. You will see that there is only one 'desirable' element, but clearly relevant work experience is, as usual, very attractive to an employer.

As not many graduates will have worked in publishing before, you should still apply if you want the job and meet the essential criteria.

➢ Degree – good science degree, ideally with a large chemical component

➢ Computing – Microsoft Office and email

➢ A wide range of transferable skills

➢ Understanding of the term STM (Scientific, Technical and Medical)

➢ Also, any experience of publishing or editing/proof-reading etc. (don't forget essays, dissertation etc.)

They will also expect you to show motivation towards living in the area (this is a Cambridge company), going into scientific publishing, spending time with journals and databases, editing and correcting documents and becoming an editor.

Job Description

Job purpose

This is a great opportunity to work with dynamic journal teams and academics to ensure the company publishes leading journals and databases for the chemical science community worldwide. You will be a critical part of the whole publishing process from initial submission through to final publication.

Essential skills and qualifications

- A good honours degree in science is essential (chemical science normally preferred)
- Good organizational and time-management skills are required together with the ability to work under pressure, prioritize and meet deadlines
- Good attention to detail
- A proactive approach to problem solving is required
- Good communication skills in interacting with internal and external contacts are essential
- Proven ability to work well in a team
- Experience using standard email and Microsoft Office packages

Desirable skills and qualifications

Postgraduate experience and/or practical experience in STM publishing would be an asset.

In-depth analysis

Opposite is a job description for an HR graduate trainee post analysed in detail:

Skills, qualifications, experience and personal qualities

1 Find out what CIPD stands for and what is involved in this Human Resources qualification.

2 Evidence of a degree – no subject specified so all should be acceptable but there could be an advantage in stressing any content related to planning, construction, environmental issues etc.

3 Have you had any work or industry experience? Even a few months is important to specify, especially for this job as Human Resources is relevant to all employees in all sectors.

HUMAN RESOURCES GRADUATE TRAINEE FOR CAPITAL WORKS, REGENERATION AND SUPPORT SERVICES COMPANY
(Building schools, houses, offices and hotels)

Essential Qualifications
- Degree or equivalent

Desirable Qualifications
- Achieved or working towards CIPD
- Good written and numeracy skills
- Successfully worked as part of a team
- Managing varied administrative tasks
- Being analytical and forward thinking
- Attention to detail and completer finisher
- Clear and concise communication skills
- Able to work as part of an effective team
- Working unassisted and using initiave to organize workload

Desirable Skills
Working towards appropriate professional membership

Desirable Experience
Significant experience of working in an office environment

Personal Qualities
Self awareness
You will be able to:
- reflect regularly on your own experiences and performance, and constantly seek to improve
- model behaviour that shows respect, helpfulness and co-operation

Relationship Focused
You will be able to:
- recognize the importance of relationships and build these across the organization
- identify your customers' needs and expectations and strive to deliver them

Delivering Objectives
You will be able to:
- constructively challenge the status quo and seek better alternatives
- take personal responsibility for makin things happen
- find practical ways to overcome barriers
- manage multiple demands without loosing focus or energy

4 Are you working towards CIPD, or have you achieved a Personnel and Development qualification? If not, do you have experience or qualifications in relevant areas such as training, coaching, mentoring, e-learning, employment law, mergers and acquisitions and other corporate strategies? If not, it is worth specifying that you understand what it covers and would be very keen to study for the qualification.

5   Evidence of working with Word, Excel, Access, PowerPoint etc. If not, have you worked with Open Office or similar software?

6   Evidence of written skills – try to find these from as wide a source as possible, e.g. degree course, work experience, leisure, family situations etc. Business (emails, memos, reports), online, leisure fiction and non-fiction writing should all be mentioned.

7   Evidence of numeracy skills – again, find these widely unless you can offer high-level mathematical qualifications, e.g. GCSE, in your degree course, handling money or analysing statistics, being a finance officer etc.

8   Teamwork – look for examples of group activities and team membership.

9   Admin – can you point to any administrative roles such as filing, answering the telephone, database management, any office work, budgeting, report writing, or membership of any committees?

10 Analytical and forward-thinking – do you have evidence from your degree, from jobs, from courses or in your hobbies or social life? Most degree work involves some analysis, e.g. of papers, findings, arguments etc.

11 Attention to detail and finishing – do you always complete work such as projects, reports, experiments etc., and do you have evidence that you pay attention to detail, e.g. proof-reading, editing, counting, recording, observing, craftwork etc.?

12 Communication skills – this is apart from writing (number 6), so could include speaking, listening, instructing, teaching, coaching, acting, etc.

13 Team working – covered at number 8.

14 Self-directed, initiator – evidence from organizing your own time-table, workload, running clubs, setting up things like an online business and from work experience etc. Look for evidence that

you can work well on your own without constant supervision.

15 Self-awareness – can you find examples of having analysed projects, activities etc. to identify areas for further training or improvement?

16 Cooperative and helpful – any examples from work, degree or leisure of working in this way?

17 Relationships – evidence that you build up good relationships socially, during the course, at work, in clubs and societies etc.

18 Customer focus – ideally some experience of serving customers or identifying people's needs.

19 Challenging the status quo – any examples of how you have improved things for fellow students, family members or work colleagues without appearing aggressive or a troublemaker?

20 Make things happen – similar to number 14, they want evidence of you being an initiator.

21 Overcome barriers – any in your life, e.g. had to overcome a physical disability, discrimination, dyslexia etc., or financial or personal issues?

22 To overcome barriers, you need to be a problem solver, e.g. what problems have you had to solve and how did you go about it?

23 Ability to multitask – have you juggled a number of part-time jobs plus work etc., or several projects and met all the targets and deadlines?

Interests, attitudes and working conditions

1 Indicate why you want to work in their industry and for this company – do you have experience, knowledge, thoughts on developments in this area (as you should have read their literature as well as round the subject)?

87

2   Why do you want to train in HR? You need to be very aware of what the work entails and could mention aspects such as an interest in people, their welfare at work and any legal or other relevant background or interests you have.

3   Find out about such things as where the job is based, if there is travel required etc. and confirm your pleasure or interest in working there.

4   Ambitions – this is a trainee post, so you might want to indicate which area of HR you might specialize in if it is an option.

Conclusion

If you have disadvantages, like little work experience or not studying for the qualifications they 'desire', remember that many other candidates will not have them either, and even if they do, it still may not make them a better candidate. Instead, make the most of everything else you can offer.

MAKING THE MOST OF THE WRONG JOB

It is quite likely that you may have to take one or a series of jobs you don't really want – anything from cleaning to shelf stacking, call centre work, waitressing, data entry, tutoring, retail sales, kitchen work, building site jobs etc. – to avoid unemployment. Fortunately, if the experience is not too soul-destroying and does not last too long, it can be of benefit.

Here are a few of the good points:

➢ You are in work. Applications from people in work are nearly always better than those from people who are out of work simply because it indicates you are 'employable'

EXAMPLE

Two recent graduates in philosophy and history from a shared house in one university town are currently working at Waitrose (in the café) and at Poundland (as a sales assistant). Neither of them plans to have long-term careers in retail or catering but they are both relieved to be in work.

➤ You are gaining some transferable work-related skills. These may be as simple as time-keeping, working in a team, following instructions, setting out business correspondence, answering the phone, dealing with customers/staff/clients/suppliers etc. or working with computers, machinery, the till, photocopiers, knives etc.

➤ You may gain extra qualifications, e.g. health and safety, hygiene, life-saving, catering, computing etc.

➤ You will be experiencing work of a specific type in a particular sector, e.g. hotel and catering, retail, banking, construction etc., that may provide relevant employment skills and knowledge or aid your self-awareness

➤ You should be able to get a good reference and confirmation that you are reliable, honest, easy to work with, a good team player etc.

➤ You can often progress from one of these jobs to a more responsible position within the same organization such as supervisor, trainer or assistant manager

➤ If it is a really awful job, you should be able to identify the reasons why. This will give you valuable insights that will help you when you apply for your next position

If you use the time as wisely as you can, you can make it work to your advantage in the longer-term.

EXAMPLE

I spent six months as a departmental secretary in a college, typing letters for the head of department. Near the end of my time there, I was asked to take the minutes for a series of committee meetings. When I applied for my first administrative job, my committee experience was seen as a relevant and valuable skill, as part of my new role involved acting as secretary to a number of committees.

Selecting a relevant starting point

If you have a choice and have a rough career direction in mind, try to find a job as closely related to your ultimate goal as you can so that you will have some relevant experience to offer. 'Starting from the bottom' is a common route to the top. Also, if you think short-term, part-time, low-level jobs will be your only route into your ideal career, it might be worth identifying the best types of job to apply for. One way is to create a spidergram.

1 Write down your ideal job or type of work in the centre of a piece of paper, e.g. 'Run a Restaurant', 'Boat Surveyor' or 'Airline Procurement Manager'. Think of all the skills and experiences that someone in that role might need or would find useful, and write them down round your central career idea. Join each one up to the centre by a line.

2 For each of the skills and experiences, think of a place or job where you could gain them and join it to the idea with a line.

3 Keep building up your web of ideas until you have a number of jobs that lead towards your ideal position.

4 Concentrate your job search on those types of work or employers.

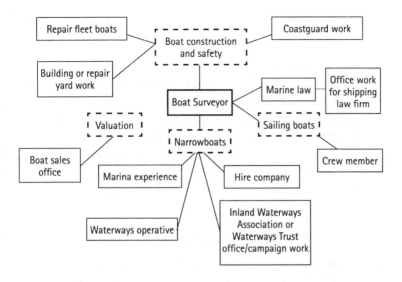

PREPARATION WORK

The next step involves applying for jobs and you may find yourself applying for a wide range of jobs that require different qualifications, experience and personal qualities. Before you can complete any forms or create your selling documentation, you will need to have all the salient facts at your fingertips. Otherwise, each time you have to fill in a new form, you will have to dig out all your details again.

Either in a box file or on the computer, start gathering together all your education, training, work and other details, along with dates, grades, titles, addresses etc., so that you can refer to them when you need to put them down in your applications.

Here are some of the things you may need:

➢ School, college/distance learning and university names and basic addresses, attendance dates, examinations taken, qualifications and grades achieved plus dates, any current study you are involved in, even if the final qualification has not yet been awarded

➢ Work – paid or unpaid – employers – names, locations and business – your roles, titles, responsibilities etc. with dates

➢ Positions of responsibility – dates, titles, roles, achievements, e.g. promotions, awards

➢ Achievements in other areas of life

➢ Leisure activities worth mentioning – those showing expertise or transferable skills like leadership or teamwork

➢ Goals – both short and longer-term

SUMMARY

1 Once you understand what employers want, it is much easier to prepare your applications.

2 Take care to analyse job advertisements carefully so that you address every single capability or personal trait that is being asked for.

3 Use every resource to find out as much as possible about the work and the employer before applying.

4 Make sure you stress that you have all the essential qualities and as many desirable ones as you can.

5 Always provide evidence for every statement you make.

6 If you have to take on jobs that don't interest you, try to get the most out of them and choose carefully so that you can use them as a stepping stone towards your ultimate goal.

MAKING APPLICATIONS

This step is divided into three sections: finding jobs to apply for; making an application; and what to do while you wait.

RULES FOR SUCCESSFUL JOB HUNTING

Unfortunately, hundreds of other candidates will be applying for the same jobs as you, whatever route you take, so you need to make sure your application is successful.

Here are three golden rules to follow:

1 Don't apply for jobs that are clearly unsuitable – either because you cannot do them or you wouldn't want them. This is a recipe for wasting time and feeling negative about yourself when you are rejected.

2 Be fully prepared for the application process – this includes doing your homework and being able to provide evidence that you are the most suitable candidate. See 'Step 4 – Getting Ready to Apply' for further help.

3 If you are fairly desperate for any job, still do as much preparation as possible before you apply so that you appear to be the most suitable and well-motivated candidate. Only then will you have the best chance of receiving a job offer.

To follow the rules, you have to know as much about yourself as you can. Self-awareness will:

➤ Help you target your applications in the most appropriate directions

➤ Allow you to make informed decisions about whether a job you find out about is likely to be suitable

➤ Help you prepare your applications so that you have the best chance of success

Following the rules also means that you have to understand exactly what the employers are looking for.

It is worth remembering that many graduates take jobs that are completely unrelated to their preferred or final career destination, usually jobs that do not require a degree, for a variety of reasons including making some money and giving themselves time to think about what they want to do. They still need to take care with their applications as they could be spending up to a year or more in that first position, and the lower the level of work, the more potential candidates there will be who can compete successfully against them.

WHERE TO HEAR ABOUT JOBS

There are a number of different ways you might hear about work or could encourage employers to think about employing you, including:

1 Word of mouth – being told about a job before it is advertised. This could be through family and friends or by using official and unofficial networks.

2 Using agencies and online job lists, including student union job shops and the Jobcentre Plus online website 'Universal Jobmatch'.

3 Looking through newspapers and journals.

4 Spotting cards in shop windows or on noticeboards.

5   Starting as a temp or volunteer and finding out about vacancies within your own organization – by word of mouth or their Intranet.

6   Going on a placement or internship.

7   Attending university-organized events such as the Milkround and job fairs.

8   Visiting organizations' own websites.

9   Making a speculative application – approaching employers without knowing first if they have any work available.

NETWORKING

As a student, you are probably well aware of the power of the 'grapevine' when it comes to finding out about parties, gigs or other private events that are never officially advertised. The grapevine, or word of mouth, is just as powerful in the world of job hunting, so as well as looking at official job advertisements or attending public recruiting events, try to make the most of any informal opportunities to locate work that you come across.

Many jobs are never advertised. Certainly at middle- to senior-management levels, you might expect that recruitment often takes place via headhunters or people being sought through recommendations and business contacts. Nowadays it can be a viable alternative for graduate job hunters to use networking systems too.

Networking can also be a way to find out useful information. Many large employers use Facebook or other sites to put up material aimed at graduates, so use these as well as conventional company websites, and follow individuals on Twitter to see what they are saying about relevant issues. You might also find it worth using www.twitjobsearch.com as it allows you to search Twitter for specific posts or internships.

When you attend events in person, take along your own business cards, which you can create freely or very cheaply on a computer, ready to hand round if and when it is appropriate. Although the ideal may be a job, networking is a good way to find out about shadowing or work-experience opportunities too, as well as simply discuss careers with people who can offer valuable advice or suggest new contacts to follow up. It should be noted that it can be 'bad form' to ask outright for a job. Instead, think of networking as a way of making useful contacts, building a growing list of names of people you can talk to about work and who might hear of opportunities you could apply for.

Groups both off and online are worth making the most of, and here are just a few:

Alumni associations

Use your university alumni association (set up within every institution as a means by which they keep in touch with graduates and raise money) to make contact with former students who are now in organizations or who are doing jobs that appeal to you. They are usually very happy to help current students and may either chat on the telephone or agree to meet.

Membership of professional bodies

Many of the professional bodies that cover careers as diverse as engineering, computing and publishing have young members groups, which organize events. You can socialize and network with people in the same industry or business. For example, according to the Institute of Mechanical Engineers:

> For a few hours of your time a month, you can develop personally and professionally whilst contributing to a very worthwhile and rewarding activity.
>
> • Meet industry professionals
> • Learn from other young engineers

- Locally and nationally influence the direction of your professional body
- Improve your career prospects

Round Table or Ladies Circle

These are national and international networks of clubs for men and women who meet to socialize and have fun, help their community, develop new skills and build contacts. For both clubs, the age range is eighteen to forty-five. The Round Table is for men, and events that you could get involved in include karting, beer festivals, skydiving, hiking or bike rides. There are over 250 Ladies Circle clubs and they offer anything from fashion shows to white-water rafting. Before joining, you can go along to a couple of meetings to find out if it would suit you. Full details of all the clubs can be found at www. roundtable.co.uk or www.ladiescircle.co.uk.

Meetup

This is a noticeboard at www.meetup.com for clubs around the country who have put their details online. Enter the name of your local town or county and you will find clubs and societies that may be of interest. Exeter, for example, lists a group called Exeter-Web made up of designers, developers, marketers, animators, copywriters, photographers and others who work on the Web; Bristol has SWmobile that aims to help connect anyone in the business of making mobile apps, and the Newcastle group NEcreative is for anyone interested in the creative industries.

LinkedIn

The social network website www.linkedin.com was set up in 2003 for the purpose of helping business people develop their professional relationships. Members create their pages based on their work and education record rather than leisure pursuits or social friendships, and once they publish their skills and experience, recruiters can search for and contact them about work so that experienced workers often don't even need to apply for a job. It is a good place for members to create an aura of expertise as well, as they can reply to questions posted on discussion boards and forums or make intelligent comments.

As a job seeker you can use the site to help in your job search in a variety of ways. For example, you can set up your own profile, emphasizing particular skills or achievements and even upload a CV, and you can search for:

- Named individuals in particular organizations or people doing specific jobs, either to target with speculative applications or just to make contact and ask for advice

- Answers to work-related queries

- Potential contacts with whom you already have something in common, if you see they are a member of any alumni group or organization you have been involved with

- Contact details of friends or colleagues of someone in a company of interest; they may be worth contacting if they are in your target organization or line of work

- Someone who can help you learn more about a type of job or organization, even if they no longer work there, by checking their listed previous types of work or employers

- Up-to-date contact details for people you want to send applications to, to make sure they still work in a particular organization and that you address them correctly

- Advertised jobs. By clicking the Jobs link and selecting 'Find Jobs', you can put in the usual criteria such as keywords and location and follow up any vacancies.

Networking drawbacks

Unfortunately, as well as you using networks to find jobs, you may now find that many employers are using them to find *you*. So if you have daft pictures of yourself on Facebook, make negative comments on Twitter, write angry blogs or posts or otherwise present yourself in a not-very-flattering light online, it may come to your potential employer's attention and work against you.

The best things to do include:

➤ Changing your privacy settings so that only close friends can view your personal details

➤ Don't put anything up there that could embarrass you – delete unwanted old material if you can

➤ Start work on a professional profile, e.g. on LinkedIn using your real name so that business-like material promoting your positive experience or skills will be found if anyone does a search

➤ Set up your own blog. You can put across views and comments that show you in the most positive light, and also showcase any relevant work or ideas

WEBSITES AND AGENCIES

With more organizations and companies putting their details on the Web, this is one of the most common and convenient ways to find vacancies. In some cases, there is still a high-street agency with real people to talk to, or a publication you can buy or read in the library, but all avenues should be fully explored.

Company websites

When you know you want to work for your local council, for a water company in the north-east or with a software engineering company in Swindon, the best place to go to online is their own website.

Here you will find the latest vacancies, details of the application procedures and any downloadable application forms. You may even be able to apply directly by completing an online form or uploading your CV.

Agencies and job lists

First of all, make sure you visit your university careers service and student union job shop regularly as they are often a good place to learn about suitable vacancies, internships or campus jobs and the staff will have lots of advice, support and help to offer.

With the commercial agencies, such as Reed, Monster, Total Jobs, Simply Hired or Target Jobs, signing on with an agency or registering or searching an online jobsite is free. Some sites deal exclusively with certain types of employment such as publishing, advertising, editing and proof-reading or the catering trade. For example: Drapers (fashion jobs), eFinancial careers, PropertyWeek4Jobs and Insurance Times, as well as sites for jobs in museums (www.museumjobs.com), academic posts (www.jobs.ac.uk) and newspapers (www.holdthefrontpage.co.uk).

Sites for cities starting 'This Is . . .' list jobs in a wide range of towns and cities if you want to work in a particular place. There are now also a number of websites that cater especially for graduate jobs and placements, including Gradplus, the Graduate Recruitment Company, Graduate-jobs, Inside careers, Milkround and Prospects.

Do not expect high-street agencies to put themselves out for you. If you are vague about what type of work you want, they won't be much help as they are not careers advisers. Use them as only part of your job-search strategy and make sure your CV is top quality and includes a very clear personal statement about the type of work you are looking for and what you have to offer, in case they lose it or don't want a covering letter. You can often set up an email alert so that you hear about new jobs that fit your requirements as soon as they are posted.

National and regional newspaper websites are worth checking, including the *Guardian*, *Daily Telegraph* and places like the *Bolton News*, Brighton's *Argus* or Bournemouth's *Daily Echo*. There is also the government's Universal Job Match at jobsearch.direct.gov.uk .

It is worth noting that, if you want to work locally, the print version of a local newspaper's jobs pages is often far easier to browse regularly than the online equivalents. Trying to put the right criteria in the boxes can still end up with an unmanageable number of jobs that are hard to filter. Skimming a page of adverts is often far quicker.

Trades and professions

As well as looking in your local paper, most trades and professions are linked to associations or institutes and they all produce journals and magazines. These normally include a classified section offering specialist posts and there may be more vacancy details on their websites, or they may even be exclusively online. Examples include *PR Week*, *Marketing Week*, the *Timber Trade Journal*, *The Grocer*, *Horticulture Week* and *Retail Week*.

INTERNSHIPS

These are fixed-term and supervised work placements that, nowadays, usually pay and can last from a few weeks to up to a year. The shorter placements are usually available during your time at university, in the summer at the end of your penultimate year, but different schemes are also available when you graduate. The experience you gain and contacts you make during your time on these schemes can help you find a permanent job as they are often in sought-after areas of work that are extremely hard to enter directly, such as fashion, journalism, marketing, publishing, travel, buying or design.

As well as fashion and marketing-type positions, internships are available within many of the more conventional areas that graduates enter directly, such as business, administration, engineering, finance or human resources and are offered by large numbers of blue-chip companies. The advantage to companies of internships over graduate training schemes is that they can find out about you without the commitment of an offer of work. Often, it will lead to a job at the end of the placement but that is their choice.

Many universities run internship schemes as they receive funding from sources such as the European Regional Development Fund, so you should always check if your own university can help find you a placement. You can also use the Graduate Talent Pool (run by the Department of Business, Innovation and Skills), or agencies such as www.inspiringinterns.com, www.e4s.co.uk, www.internwise.co.uk or www.milkround.com. Even standard online recruitment agencies can list vacancies on internship schemes.

It should be noted that some 'internships' are actually more like part-time or voluntary work. For example, one charity was recently offering a 'Corporate Giving Volunteer Internship' that only paid lunch money and expenses and lasted four weeks.

MILKROUND AND JOB FAIRS

Details of the final-year Milkround should be well publicized by your careers service. If you missed taking part, or were unsuccessful, many universities also put on jobs fairs later in the year, where you can have another chance to meet employers and talk to them about work. For example, London University ran graduate fairs in June and October 2012 and January (for postgraduate study) and March 2013.

Prepare carefully, so that you:

➤ Look smart and appear highly motivated

➤ Are ready for an instant interview

➤ Take notes of names, contact details and any useful information

➤ Book a place early on seminars or workshops

➤ Have enough copies of your CV to hand out, bearing in mind the personal statement may need to be removed or 'generalized'

➤ Take a bag or briefcase for all the brochures you will pick up

➤ Have some business cards made out, if a CV is not appropriate

➤ Remember you are on show and they may take a note of your details – only ask sensible and intelligent questions

➤ Practise a firm but not bone-crunching handshake, and speak your name and answer questions clearly and directly

SPECULATIVE APPLICATIONS

'Having your details on file' can often turn out to be surprisingly successful as a job-hunting tactic. If you have made a strong case for yourself, you meet most of the organization's requirements and they have a reasonable turnover of staff, just because there is no job available for you at the time you contact them doesn't mean there never will be. It often happens that, some months after you send in your application, someone will ring you and ask if you are still free.

It is a good idea to keep your eye on the local paper. If a shop, factory, head office or other establishment plans to open in your area, you can then be the first to send in a speculative letter asking about upcoming vacancies.

See below for what to put in your letter of application.

BASIC RULES FOR APPLYING

Everyone seems to have a view about how to write a CV or fill in an application form, but there really isn't a perfect template that you can use. Read all the suggestions and examples in this Step and then choose the way that suits you best.

Making an application is usually the first time a potential employer will have any contact with you. From this moment on, everything you do must be aimed at making the best impression. This includes how you speak on the phone, what you put in writing and your behaviour when you visit the organization.

With that in mind, think about your handwriting, the way you set out documents, the paper and envelopes you use, the name you want to be called by, your contact details and your email address.

As an example, what impression would an application make from juicyfruit@hotmail.com? Fortunately, it is extremely easy to set up a new email address where you can use your own name and – if you want to – you can keep it just for the length of time it takes to find a job.

Try to word process as much as you can, especially if your handwriting is poor, and keep everything ink-free, carefully checked for grammar and spelling mistakes and printed on good-quality plain white paper. (Gimmicks or unusual methods for making your application 'stand out', such as holographic paper or pop-up models, may work for some people, or when you are applying for a few of the jobs in the creative industries, but for the majority of new graduates it is probably not a risk worth taking. If you believe you have a good idea for an original approach and want to use it, try to run it past someone who can offer credible advice.)

Why a CV through the door is not enough

On some occasions, and particularly when applying online, you may not be able to do anything other than send in your CV. Unfortunately, it alone is really not enough to get a job interview. Even with a personal statement at the top, it is usually only a summary of your education and training, work experience and other supporting information such as publications, overseas experience or relevant leisure activities and achievements.

Unless you want to write a new CV every single time you apply for a job, it will not answer those crucial questions in the minds of recruiters:

➤ Can you do this particular job?

➤ What can you offer?

➤ Do you really want this job and/or to work for us?

➤ Will you fit in and progress as we would wish you to?

This means that dropping a CV on its own through the letterbox of any office, factory or company headquarters, sending it by email with a brief message about the target vacancy, or leaving it at reception or with a member of the sales staff and asking them to 'pass it on' is not good enough.

Instead, you have to use the CV as backup for your covering letter.

EXAMPLE

Imagine you are applying for one of three jobs featured earlier:

– Teaching Assistant
– Librarian
– Human Resources graduate trainee

Your CV shows you have worked as a Saturday sales assistant at a local newsagent, were a member of the fencing team and have a degree in botany. There is not enough room to put down everything you have done in your life, and yet a few activities not likely to be featured in any depth (if at all) might be vitally relevant:

a   Helping to bring up a younger disabled brother (the Teaching Assistant job involves working one-to-one with a disabled child

CONTINUED

---

b   Helping catalogue your grandfather's collection of butter-
flies and moths when he moved house and showing him
how to use Microsoft Access to set up a database (both
relevant to the Library and Teaching Assistant positions)

c   Spending a few days at a head office shadowing a Human
Resources Manager when she was negotiating a new pay
deal – helping to explain your motivation towards the
Human Resources post. (If you spent time in a variety of
departments, your CV might only mention the overall
programme briefly.)

It is in your covering letter that you pull out and feature
details such as these that would be hidden or even missing
from a general CV.

The best way to sell yourself

Applying for jobs is like taking part in any competition – you want
to beat the other competitors and win the prize. To do this, you have
to be honest *but* present yourself in the best possible light. Here are
five rules to follow:

- Don't tell lies. Lying is never a good idea and with applications
there are usually consequences. For example, if you claim qualifications you don't have, gained a third-class degree and put down
that it was actually a 2:1, or were fired but say you chose to leave
a job, it probably won't take long for the employer to find out
from your referees or through their research and they will then
know that you are dishonest.

- Address an employer's underlying fears. For example, if you had
a breakdown or have a disability that will need to be addressed

at work, try to describe these things in a positive way. Despite recent legislation making discrimination illegal, employers will still worry that you cannot cope with the job. Allay their fears by stressing that, although things happened to you in the past, you are now coping well and could perform all the tasks expected of you.

- Make the most of your experiences. If you failed an examination or gave up a course of study and yet the content of the course was relevant, stress the knowledge you gained without emphasizing the failure. And if you had to leave a job after only a short while, again, emphasize the things you learned during your time there. Obviously, if you made a contribution, this should be highlighted.

- Don't feel obliged to tell the whole truth. There is no rule that says you have to put down everything, and that certainly applies to negative information, such as failing a driving test five times or not getting on with anyone on your course. This also applies to any bad experiences during a temporary job or as a volunteer. If it doesn't leave a large gap in time unaccounted for and the experience is not relevant to the role you are applying for, you can simply leave out things that show you in a poor light.

- Don't 'talk up' your experience or expertise. Everyone knows what it means to be a school prefect or club secretary, so don't boast and try to make out that your role was far more important than it was or you will just end up looking silly. Being positive is not the same as being a fantasist.

COVERING LETTERS

Whenever possible, you should send a well-thought-out covering letter with any application. When sent with a CV, it should summarize your suitability for the post and wet the recruiter's appetite for further information. Never lose an opportunity to sell yourself so do not simply write a sentence saying that your CV is attached.

With the application form it can be briefer, but it still needs to tell them which post you are applying for and why they should consider you, even though the form itself will go into more details about motivation and suitability.

Covering letter with a CV

As you will already have read, it is here that you bring out the very specific capabilities, experience and knowledge that make you the best person for the job. Even if there is a reasonable amount of detail about certain experiences in your CV, you still need to summarize them in the covering letter just to make sure they are not overlooked. Where important information for this job is hidden, omitted or underplayed in a concise CV, you must make sure you get it across in your letter.

Each time you sit down to apply for a job, ask yourself:

■ What makes you a strong candidate? Do you have the right educational qualifications, relevant work experience, valuable transferable skills, personal qualities they are looking for or something special you can bring to the job? You will need to set these out clearly in a couple of paragraphs.

■ Why do you want this particular job? Perhaps it is because it looks fun, it pays well, it is near to home, you can use your past experience, it ties in with your values, they are offering opportunities for further training or it is something you have always wanted to do. Whatever the reasons, try to summarize them in a way that would most appeal to the employer and show them that you are fully aware of what the job will be.

Some organizations have lots of advertisements out at the same time, so when you apply for any job or training scheme, make sure you tell them:

➢ Which position you are applying for and, if relevant, where you saw the advert and any reference numbers

As well as:

➢ What you can offer

➢ Why you want the job

➢ What you are sending to them

➢ Any further information they might need

Usually, a covering letter would be no more than one page in length, but if you have to go onto a second page, always number your pages.

There are conventions for business letters and so this letter should have:

1   Your name and address at the top:
    Stephanie Coombs
    23 Worsley Avenue
    Manchester, M28 3PW
    Tel: 0161 33240067

2   The name, job title and address of the person you are sending your CV to, usually left-aligned:
    Ms Fiona Ross
    PA to the Housing Manager
    Leeds Local Authority
    Wrackham Road
    Leeds
    LS29 4AP

3   The date.

4   The greeting, e.g. 'Dear Ms Ross' or (if no name is provided) 'Dear Sir/Madam'.

5   The subject, i.e. job details (emphasized), e.g. Housing Support Officer (Ref: HL2304).

6   The main body of your letter:

a   Why you are writing, e.g. 'I would like to apply for the post of Housing Support Officer advertised recently in the *Leeds Herald*.'

b   What you have to offer, e.g. 'Since leaving Durham University with a degree in History, I have been working as a part-time lettings agent with Fox and Sons. As you will see from my CV, this has involved writing copy for the weekly property newsletter and showing potential purchasers round properties. I also prepare inventories for landlords and update the computer records on a regular basis. At university, I worked as a volunteer in the student union accommodation office and so I feel I have a lot of experience to offer.
'I gained excellent customer service skills through a part-time sales job at Marks & Spencer and am computer literate with several years' experience in Microsoft Office applications. I also hope to pass my driving test in the next few weeks.'

c   Why you want the job, e.g. 'I really enjoy my lettings work but, as so many landlords are not interested in tenants on housing benefit, I would prefer to work in the public sector where the main focus is on helping vulnerable members of society find accommodation. I am particularly interested in the Housing Support Office post as you are offering the chance to gain membership of the Chartered Institute of Housing.'

d   What you are sending and anything extra they need to know, e.g. 'I enclose my CV and look forward to hearing from you. For your information, I will be on holiday between 7 and 14 July.'

7 Your ending – 'Yours sincerely' for a named person; 'Yours faithfully' if you only know the job title. Leave a gap for your signature and then type your name.

8 If you type 'Encl.' at the bottom, this confirms there should be enclosures or attachments.

9 Before posting it, check that all enclosures are there. Don't staple the letter to the CV, but you can attach it with a paperclip. If they have asked for several copies of your CV, make sure you have included them all.

Covering letter by email

As this has exactly the same purpose as a normal covering letter, all you need do is change the following details:

1 Keep the greeting formal, e.g. 'Dear Ms Ross' or 'Fiona Ross'.

2 There will be no address details or dates to add, but you could include a phone number at the end, under your name, if you want to. If you are applying legitimately from work, you may want to keep the business signature you normally use.

3 Put the details of the post as the email subject.

4 Include just the same content as 6 a–d above, but 'attach' rather than 'enclose' the CV.

5 You won't include a 'Yours sincerely' so just end with your full name.

6 Check for errors and that the CV is actually attached before clicking send.

Covering letter with an application form

This should have the same layout as a letter sent with a CV and can include a brief summary of sections 6 b and c above to stress your particular suitability for the post.

SPECULATIVE LETTERS SENT WITH A CV

Writing to organizations without knowing if they have any vacancies is normal, accepted practice and can be very successful. The only problem for you as an applicant is that you don't have any specific job to apply for so will have fewer clues as to what they might be looking for. It is up to you to:

➢ Research the sector
➢ Research the type of organization
➢ Research the type of work that interests you
➢ Research the actual roles this organization is likely to have
➢ Try to find a named person to write to. (If you cannot do that, write 'Dear Sir/Madam')
➢ Be positive but not pushy

Who to write to

If there are a number of organizations of a similar type that take graduates (e.g. advertising agencies, accountancy firms, breweries etc.), but you want to write to one that is not coming to the Milk-round or advertising anywhere, then you can send the same sort of application you would send to all the others and your careers service may have full contact details for the graduate recruitment manager. Unless they provide a general application form on their website, you are going to need to send a letter with a CV. If you don't have a name, phone the organization and try to find the name and/or job title of the appropriate person.

With firms or organizations not on the usual Milkround circuit, you need to write to someone with the power to create openings. If your target position fits within a particular department or section, it might be better to write to the head of that rather than a general recruitment or personnel department.

If it is a small, little-known organization, you will have to tailor your letter more carefully and would probably write to the manager, owner or head of the relevant department. Again, phone up to try to get the right name and title.

Content

There are two or three ways in which speculative letters will differ from covering letters sent with CVs: contact details if these are likely to change over the next few months, and the introductory and end paragraphs. The main part of the letter should be very similar to normal covering letters sent with CVs.

You need to tell them:

➢ Any contact detail changes if these are coming up
➢ The sort of work you want to do
➢ That you look forward to hearing from them if vacancies arise

Your reasons for applying will be similar to those you give for an advertised job, for example:

1 The area of work is one where you have experience, skills or proven interest.
2 They offer jobs you are trained to carry out.
3 You have a connection with the organization.
4 Their organization is of special interest to you.

Your first sentence could be along the following lines:

I am keen to use my art qualifications and graphical illustration skills to work in the advertising industry. Your company is a market leader in digital advertising and I am writing to ask if you have any vacancies for junior design staff.

The more specific you can be about your preferred role, the easier it will be to prepare a suitable profile on your CV and include the relevant details in both the CV and your covering letter. If you are really willing to do anything just to get a job with them, take care that you don't come across as too unfocused and vague, or lacking enough evidence for statements about your strengths and capabilities.

I have seen lots of letter endings including phrases like: 'I am able to come to interviews at any time', 'I will be delighted to discuss any possible vacancy with you at your convenience' or 'thank you for taking the time to consider this application', which all seem quite unnecessary.

Personally, I prefer a simple ending: 'I enclose my CV and look forward to hearing from you if you have any suitable vacancies now or in the future.'

CURRICULUM VITAE

The CV (or résumé) is the background document you create that sets out your qualifications, skills, experience and personal qualities. This section provides a summary of the basic approach to designing your CV, and if you want to see lots of examples of different CVs there are pages of these on the internet.

If you think about how many hundreds of CVs each recruiter will receive, your task is simply to show that:

➢ You meet the essential criteria

➢ You meet some or all of the desirable criteria

➢ It is aimed at their organization and, ideally, their job

➢ You are clearly keen to work for them

➢ You have taken the trouble to set your details out professionally

➢ It is easy to read

➢ It is easy to navigate

➢ There is just the right amount of information – no more and no less

➤ You haven't provided them with an old document that is no longer relevant

As everything you do when applying for jobs should be aimed at making life easier for recruiters, this must also apply to your CV.

Why CVs get rejected

Clearly, any candidate who doesn't have the right qualifications for a post will be rejected out of hand, but that still leaves a large number who could do the job and yet are not called in for an interview. To make sure your CV doesn't end up in the reject pile, avoid producing a document that:

1   Is too long or too short. Limit the length of your CV to two to three sides of A4 paper if you can. Fewer than two pages and you are probably leaving out too much relevant information about roles, activities, responsibilities, qualifications, coursework etc. Over three pages and, even if you are incredibly experienced, you are probably including far too much detail that is not required. Apply the 'so what?' rule to everything you include. If details you put down add nothing – and for mature students this often takes the form of redundant data far in the past such as school or college material or various part-time jobs that have been left in because you haven't done the pruning each time your CV is updated – cut them out.

2   Doesn't sell you fast enough. Get the salient points across early. With limited time, don't ask recruiters to read through to the last paragraph to see that you have relevant experience or something really special to offer them. This is where a clear personal statement at the start can be so helpful.

3   Is more about what you want, not what you can offer. Applicants obviously want the job, so stressing how much you want it is a

complete waste of time and is not the same thing as evidence showing your motivation. Your main task is to show the recruiter what you can offer in terms of track record, qualifications, skills or personal qualities.

4   Is messy, poorly presented or full of errors. It is really easy for your eye to skip over mistakes when you have been working on a document for a while; you automatically visualize what you thought you had written. Before sending off any paperwork, leave it for a day or two and then read through it again carefully. If you can, ask a friend to check it as well. Take particular care with:

   a   Spelling
   b   Initial capital letters
   c   Use of apostrophes
   d   Layout – use headings and bullet points for clarity

5   Hasn't been based on seeing things from the recruiter's viewpoint. They have a role for you in mind, so all your efforts must be geared towards proving you meet their requirements. Just because amazing things have happened to you in life, don't include them if they are irrelevant to your application.

6   Doesn't reassure the recruiter you are still the right person. After analysing the job advert or description, there may be areas where you know you are weak. Rather than ignore them and hope they won't matter, try to find relevant and convincing experience and build that into the CV instead. Reassure the recruiter that you can still carry out the tasks or have enough experience.

EXAMPLE

If they want someone with 'professional editing experience' that you don't have, stress the editing skills you do have, perhaps developed through writing summaries of research findings, having music gig reviews published, using audio editing software or working on a club newsletter where you had to condense contributors' copy to fit the pages.

---

7 Is not appropriate. As long as you are applying for very similar types of position, you can probably use the same CV, provided you write separate covering letters. As soon as you think of applying for a different type of job, edit or rewrite your CV so that it is always carefully tailored to the work and/or employment sector.

8 Doesn't make it clear you have the right to work in the UK. If you are a foreign national, make sure you note somewhere in your letter or CV that you are eligible to work here. You are trying to save recruiters' time, so expecting them to chase you for this sort of information won't be helpful.

The basics

The wonderful thing about a CV, as compared to an application form, is that you choose what goes into it. You can write your own headings, group information in whatever way you like and don't have to put down anything you don't want to. If a common section is irrelevant, you can even leave it out altogether. Just remember, most recruiters will expect CVs to contain the same type of information so take care if you are going outside the norm.

As the choice of subheadings for the different sections of your CV is up to you, you may want to stick to 'Profile', 'Key Skills', 'Work Experience' and 'Interests', or go for 'Strengths', 'Key Qualifications',

'Career History', 'Work Skills', 'Areas of Expertise', 'Major Achievements', 'Vision', 'Future Plans' or any other preferred wording. It is your choice as long as overall you provide clear and adequate information.

It will be expected that your CV includes the following:

➢ Contact details, such as postal address, phone number(s) and email address. They must all be current and 'manned', i.e. if an employer tries to contact you, you will know and can respond

➢ A personal statement or profile summing up what you can offer, together with your career objectives

➢ Key skills – new graduates, especially with little work experience, need to present a summary of their key skills and experiences as they cannot rely on lots of on-the-job expertise

➢ Education and training – from secondary school (unless you went to university very late) to university, any training courses, all qualifications and dates. The amount of detail will depend on relevance

➢ Work record – include paid and unpaid work, shadowing, placements, voluntary roles etc.

➢ Anything else relevant to the jobs you are applying for such as:

- Positions of responsibility
- Achievements and successes
- Interests – as long as they show you in a positive light or relate to evidence of skills or traits they are looking for
- Contributions to society; extra section(s) as required

For new graduates, it is usual to order your CV as above and even to cut right down on the work experience part if you have little or nothing to include here. If you have years of work experience or you are in a good position currently, you may prefer to emphasize your major selling points first or start with what you are doing now.

Updating

Don't get caught out if a job you want to apply for suddenly appears. Update your CV every time you learn or do something new so that you always have the most up-to-date version available, and keep copies near to hand so you can send them off quickly.

Organization

As long as the information is presented clearly, you can organize your CV how you like. Although there are conventions with CVs, you don't have to follow any of these or you can combine the best elements if they fit your background and how you want to sell yourself.

The two most common styles have a different emphasis:

▪ **Chronological** – this is information in each section, particularly education and training and work experience, set out in date order, usually with the most recent details first (unless your most relevant experience came earlier). The problem here is that, when it comes to important aspects such as achievements, skills or experiences you may be duplicating the information across a number of courses or jobs and this may lessen their impact.

▪ **Functional** – here the main emphasis is on skills and experience regardless of where they were gained, and the dates and institutions are listed briefly somewhere later in the CV.

Reasons for choosing each style:

Chronological is often better if you:

➢ Have a strong education record
➢ Have held a number of different and interesting posts that you want to highlight in some detail
➢ Don't feel comfortable emphasizing your key skills
➢ Don't have gaps in your work or education record to worry about

119

EXAMPLE – chronological CV

Name

Contact details

Personal statement/Profile

Skills
- Team player: brief note
- Communication: brief note
- Initiative: brief note
- Computing: brief note

Education and Training

2009–2012	X University
Qualifications	BA in XXX (2:2)
Course details:	

2007–2009	X College, Town
Qualifications	A-level X, Y, Z

2004 –2007	X School, Town
Qualifications	8 GCSEs including . . .

Work Experience

2011–2012	Entertainments Officer, Student Union
	Details

2010–2012	Waitrose, Town
	Part time . . .

2008–2009	X Hospital
	Volunteer . . .

Interests

Interest 1	Details
Interest 2	Details

Additional Information

Functional or skills-based may be better if you want to:

➤ Bring your work-related and/or transferable skills to the fore

➤ Try to disguise gaps

➤ Minimize a weak education or work record

➤ Appear unconventional

EXAMPLE – functional or skills-based CV

Name
Contact details

Personal statement/Profile

Skills

Skill 1	Skill 2
• Example 1	• Example 1
• Example 2	• Example 2
	• Example 3

Skill 3

• Example 1
• Example 2

Qualifications
Degree details
A-levels
GCSEs

Work Experience

Date	Job title and employer 1
Date	Job title and employer 2
Date	Job title and employer 3

Interests

Additional Information

ACTIVITY 20

1 Decide how you think you would prefer to organize your own CV.

2 Start drafting out the main sections.

3 Work on it as you go through this book.

Using the right words

Wherever possible, rather than saying, 'I was a . . .', describe what you have been doing using Action words. These usually end with -ing such as 'updating', 'encouraging', 'supervising', 'managing', 'organising', 'editing', 'creating' etc. (A list is available on page 24).

Although it may feel unnatural, try to use positive statements that incorporate power words conveying success, confidence, motivation and achievement when you are introducing evidence of activities and capabilities. For example, don't hesitate and say, 'I feel I am . . ' or 'I have some experience in . . .' but go straight in with comments like:

➢ Proven track record in . . .

➢ Committed to . . .

➢ Confident user of . . .

➢ Able to . . .

➢ Highly motivated in . . .

Content

Tailor the wording on your CV as far as possible to match any job-advert keywords and place these early in the text. For example, if the job requires skills such as data handling, communication and teamwork, emphasize these in the work or education sections, especially if they are not going to be mentioned separately under key skills.

2010–2012	*Assistant Information Officer, Bedfordshire County Council*
Data-handling	*– responsible for updating the Council website with the latest housing data*
Communication	*– spent time on the phone or in person encouraging staff to provide case studies for the monthly newsletter*
Editing	*– wrote copy for the website and edited the Housing Department newsletter*
Teamwork	*– worked with staff in the Housing Department organizing a one-day conference for landlords*

If you can find any achievements or successes, include them somewhere appropriate – either in a separate section or with the experience. For example:

Teamwork	*– worked with staff in the Housing Department organizing a one-day conference for landlords*
Achievement	*– my suggestion to include case studies on the website resulted in an increased visitor count of over one thousand in the first three months*

ACTIVITY 21

1 Find the details of a job you want to apply for.

2 Identify any work experience or leisure activity where you used some of the key skills specified.

3 Prepare a draft for this section of your CV using action words and including references to as many key skills as you can.

4 Are there any legitimate achievements you could include?

Contact details

Keep this section as simple and short as possible, and make sure your email address on the CV (and on your computer if you are emailing the company) is standardized.

For example:

Joanne Davison
301 Portland Place
Bristol, BS1 2AE
Tel: 0117 345123
jdavison11@gmail.com

Profile or personal statement

This is a short paragraph or two that gives you the chance to show, in a nutshell and right at the start of your CV, that you are the one for them. It needs to summarize how you meet their criteria and that what you are looking for is this particular job or at least the opportunity to work in their sector.

It is the one area where you won't include lots of supporting evidence – that comes later in the CV – but you must still take care that your words do not appear as empty or unsubstantiated statements. The profile should be based on what, in your opinion, is factual information about yourself put in the most positive way and that, if asked, you could justify it with evidence. (Thinking of it in this way should help allay any fears of appearing boastful.)

It will include similar content to that of a covering letter, although for a CV it should be much shorter. Personal statements are particularly important if you have to send off your CV without a covering letter – common when applying online or after registering with some agencies – but they are also a good way to stress your suitability for any job early in the CV.

The most natural way to write the statement is in the first person using 'I' where necessary, but you could equally well produce it in note form. Think carefully before putting this section in the third

124

person ('She is a . . .') as it reads unnaturally.

What to include:

- Who you are. For example: 'An Honours graduate with a 2:1 in Chemical Engineering and experience in Singapore on a six-month industrial placement with Shell . . .' Or: 'I am a Cardiff University graduate with a degree in History with Archaeology.'

- What you can offer. For example: 'I always pay great attention to detail and had to develop advanced mathematical modelling skills for my dissertation. During my placement I specialized in pipe-line technology and produced a report whose findings have now been incorporated into the company's new safety procedures.' Or: 'Over the past three years I have worked part-time in four different London hotels where I developed excellent customer-service skills as well as an in-depth understanding of computer room bookings. I am a hard-working and fun-loving person and all my assessments have praised my enthusiasm and ability to get on well with both guests and staff at all levels.'

- Your career aim. For example: 'I am now looking to build on my overseas experience by working with an oil company on the safety aspects of pipeline engineering in the USA or the Far East.' Or: 'I would like to use my communication and organizational skills to learn all aspects of the hotel business, perhaps special-izing eventually in HR or as a General Manager.'

ACTIVITY 22

1 Write a personal statement for a specific job you have in mind.

2 Make sure it covers the three basic aspects: who you are, what you can offer and your career aim.

Key skills

Here is where you bring together the personal qualities, knowledge and skills that the job advertisements are asking for as well as any extra transferable skills that you believe would make you more attractive as an applicant. If the website or company documentation includes the organization's core values, try to build these in as well.

ACTIVITY 23

1 Write down all the skills you personally feel you have – use the work you carried out at Step 1 and include any specified in the job descriptions you are using.

2 Now add any further transferable skills you feel you can offer, perhaps some of those listed on page 16.

3 Check any other sources for interests, personal traits or values.

4 With one particular job in mind, pick out the five to ten capabilities and personal qualities that you feel you should emphasize in your CV.

The most important skills are those specific to the job. If they need someone with knowledge of paint technology, library indexing or Adobe Photoshop, these are obviously going to come high on the list. In the same way, skills like computing, languages or driving are fairly straightforward to specify. The hard part is when you try to identify and provide evidence for 'soft' transferable skills and personal qualities.

In fiction writing, it is common to be told to 'show not tell'. This means that, instead of saying someone is 'clever', 'frightening' or 'boring', you need to find a way to show these traits by the words you use. Key skills are just the same. Instead of simply stating that you are 'a team player', 'excellent communicator', 'organized' or 'reliable', you must find a way to show it.

For each skill you are going to specify, set out evidence of using the skill or gaining the knowledge in enough detail to make it clear what was involved. Depending on how you organize your CV and how many skills you want to include, this may be the largest section or you may keep it just as a bulleted list before getting on to your education and work details.

EXAMPLE

KEY SKILLS
Team player:
- Member of a small drama group writing and acting on campus and taking two review shows to Edinburgh
- Worked with three other students to carry out research and present a joint report on herring gull breeding in South Wales
- Part-time job as sales assistant in local supermarket involved organizing holiday, till and shift rotas with my colleagues

Communication:
- Wrote a number of essays and an 8,000-word dissertation for my degree
- Acting since I was fourteen so clear speaking voice and used to talking to large audiences
- Scriptwriter of comedy sketches and currently writing a play
- Spent a term as a university ambassador, taking small groups of new students and visitors round the campus
- As a supermarket cashier, have experience dealing with customers face-to-face

---

ACTIVITY 24

1   Take at least two transferable skills or qualities you will be listing in this section of your CV.

2   Provide several pieces of evidence for each one.

Education and training

This section should include details of your record at university, secondary school, college and the other educational establishments you might have attended since the age of eleven. (Mature graduates may need to start later.) You should also include training courses and separate qualifications and skills, self-taught or gained through distance learning or on-the-job training. Edit each entry so that you only mention things that are relevant. You can always summarize where required to keep sections concise.

If you are not going to include a separate 'prizes, awards, achievements' etc. section and you held a responsible position or achieved something at school or college, add this into the appropriate section with your own subheading.

EXAMPLE

2002–2009	Stanton School, Marlow, Bucks
A-levels	English Literature (A)
	Psychology (B)
	History (B)
GCSEs	9 including Mathematics, French and IT
Voluntary work	One afternoon a week in the Sixth Form helping at a local Day Centre for the elderly.

For the university section, it depends on the type of work you are applying for whether you need to include full course details and information about projects, dissertations, field trips etc. or not. If relevant, spell them out alongside the qualifications, dates and name of the university.

If you won't be using your degree subject in future, you only need to summarize or list the various modules or units you took, but make sure you give enough information for non-specialist recruiters to be clear about your degree course. If certain aspects of the course or particular modules were relevant or provide evidence of valuable skills or experience, spell these out in more detail.

EXAMPLE

For a student going into a non-relevant job:

2009–2012   BSc Environmental Geosciences 2:1
              Durham University

Modules included Earth Sciences, Water and Climate, Fossils, Structural Geology and Sedimentary and Petroleum Systems.
A large part of the course involved mathematical modelling and I spent two months in South Africa as part of a team studying rock formations. The results formed the basis of my dissertation.

ACTIVITY 25

1   Set out your university course details as appropriate for the jobs you are applying for.

2   If you will not be continuing with your subject further, pick out any evidence of work-related or transferable skills or useful experience that you need to emphasize.

For a chronological CV you normally work backwards through time. For a functional CV you may prefer to have a special 'Qualifications' section where you cut down on the details and simplify and group qualifications and institutions together, possibly without specifying all the dates. For example:

Qualifications

Durham University 2012	BSc Environmental Geosciences 2:1
	Brief details of modules, projects etc.
Stanton School, Marlow	3 A-levels – English Literature (A)
	History (B)
	Psychology (B)
	9 GCSEs – including Mathematics,
	French and English Language

Gaps

If you dropped out for a year or so, it will probably be obvious from the dates and so it is far better to provide a simple explanation rather than hoping no one will notice. Try to put a positive spin on it if you can, e.g. 'changing to a more suitable course/institution' is more positive than 'failing to cope' on the original course.

Work experience

You may have very little to put here, or just a few low-level jobs like bar or shop work, so think more widely than paid jobs and include:

➢ All placements

➢ Any work visits/experience that lasted longer than a few hours

➢ Voluntary work in the community, at school, college or university, or 'helping out' experience in a work environment

➢ Helping a family member with their work commitments at home or their workplace

➢ Official work-shadowing where you were encouraged to find out about someone's role

Where you were involved in relevant work, you need to put in as much detail as possible about your responsibilities, experiences and the skills you developed. For other experiences where you gained few or no relevant work-related or transferable skills, you still need to include the following:

1   Name of the organization and/or an idea of the business or sector:
    E.g. Redditch General Hospital, Worcs.
    Or: The Cabin, Newsagent, Worthing, Sussex

2   The dates you were there:
    E.g. Oct–Dec 2011
    Or: 2010–2013 (one afternoon a week)

3   Your job title or role:
    E.g. Volunteer Helper
    Or: Shadowing the Frozen Food Purchasing Director
    Or: Engineering trainee on industrial placement

4   Your responsibilities – using action words where possible:
    E.g. Involved in visiting the wards to issue books, keeping an eye out for any signs of distress and helping patients where they had trouble feeding themselves or filling in any forms.
    Or: I was able to attend several meetings with suppliers, get involved in a focus group tasting a new savoury rice pack and researched and produced a report on the range of similar products supplied by the company's main rivals.

5   Skills or qualifications gained – look for any transferable skills in even the simplest roles:
    E.g. Gained an understanding of the computerized stock control system and developed my customer-service skills during time spent manning the till.

Or: Attended several in-house courses on hazardous cleaning products and computer safety.

6 Any achievements – what results did you bring about over and above your expected duties?
   • Did you improve efficiency?
   • Did you improve communication?
   • Did you increase profits?
   • Did you innovate or put forward new ideas?
   • Did you reduce expenditure etc.?

Whatever the results of your own actions, state them clearly as achievements, rather than leaving them hidden in the detail of your work duties.

EXAMPLE

Housing Department Secretary:
• Weak: responsible for taking the minutes and preparing agendas for several committees as well as editing the housing newsletter
• Strong: as secretary to the major social housing committee, I initiated the policy of sending edited highlights of the minutes to all councillors, which resulted in their increased understanding of the department's financial commitments

---

ACTIVITY 26

1 Identify one activity that belongs to the work experience section.

2 Set it out as suggested above, covering the major roles and responsibilities and, ideally, including one or more achievement.

Grouping

If you have managed to find a number of part-time or short-term jobs, they may look better if you group them into a single 'story' rather than spelling out each one. Include the basic details so that recruiters will understand what you have been doing, and mention any special skills if they are relevant.

EXAMPLE

2008–2011 A range of temporary jobs including working as a clerical officer, filing clerk and photocopier for several legal and insurance firms and delivering bread for a local bakery. On several occasions, stood in for the bakery manager and organized staff rotas.

Interests

As with all the other sections, just because you have done some interesting or unusual things in the past doesn't mean they should necessarily be included in your CV. This is a sales document, so think about what you are selling and make sure it comes out in your text. Here are some examples of why interests might be included:

➢ To emphasize transferable skills such as team player, leader, organizer, numeracy, risk-taker etc.

➢ To indicate physical strengths or stamina

➢ To show you can achieve at a high level

➢ As an example of your contribution to society

➢ To offer a different 'view' of yourself so you appear a more rounded person

➢ To show a passion for something

- To have something intriguing/interesting to talk about at the interview
- To stand out from the crowd
- As evidence of work-related skills

It is best to group similar leisure activities together so they tell a simple story, and once again stress the positive elements such as achievements or transferable skills. For example:

MUSIC
I play the flute and piano to a reasonable standard and have achieved Grade 8 in violin. My family is very musical and we give concerts when I am home. I am also a member of a university quartet 'Foursome' and we are preparing to release our first CD.

MOUNTAINEERING
I started climbing at school and joined the university club in my first year. I have climbed in about ten different countries and so far have led two expeditions – one to Nepal and the other to Wales.

REPTILES
Developed an interest in snakes and lizards and now own seven snakes including a six-foot rainbow boa. One of my hobbies is designing backgrounds for the tanks and I have also built a shelving unit and heating system that works autonomously.

If your only interests are of a less formalized kind, the sort that most people are engaged in – socializing with friends, going to the cinema, reading etc., they are probably not worth putting down. But as you may be asked questions about your life outside education and work, it is definitely worth finding at least one interest that you could talk about in some depth.

ACTIVITY 27

1 Pick out three or four major interests or leisure activities.
2 Write a summary of your involvement, level achieved and any special aspects.

Positions of responsibility

These may fit better under school or university sections, but if you want to create a separate section, think about your choices and make sure they are not of the 'milk monitor' variety. Ideally they will show recognition by others or a commitment to leading, organizing, contributing, excelling, getting involved and getting things done.

You could include dates if these are relevant, or just provide a straightforward heading and explain your role and achievements and where you were at the time.

EXAMPLE

Butler's School, Bradwell
Head of House – involved in the care and discipline of boarders and helped run the school sports day. During my tenure, it was voted the happiest house and we were awarded the prize for social cohesion.

Hull University
Secretary, Biology Department Student Committee – keeping minutes of meetings and organizing two outings a year to zoos and wildlife parks. Responsible for increasing membership by 50 per cent during my two years in the role.

ACTIVITY 28

1　Identify four different positions of responsibility.

2　If you cannot find enough, consider life at university, school, home or work and for each one complete this sentence: 'During that time I was responsible for . . .' You may find you can come up with a few more examples of 'unofficial' responsible roles that are worth including in your CV.

Achievements

As well as mentioning as many achievements as you can within the relevant education, leisure and work experience sections of your CV, you may have enough extra examples to bring them together in a separate section.

Achievements come up in application forms and interviews, so it is important to be prepared for the question. If it is a tricky area for you, perhaps because you don't feel you have anything obvious to mention, start by asking yourself slightly different questions:

➤ What are you proud of?
➤ What challenges have you faced and overcome?
➤ What actions have you taken that produced a positive outcome?
➤ Have you taught yourself anything difficult?
➤ Were you ever picked out specially and for what?
➤ How have you exerted any influence?
➤ Where have you earned particular praise?
➤ What would others say you are good at, and why?
➤ What awards, prizes or competitions have you won?

Here are some examples:

1　Being picked for a team and getting good results, e.g. selected to be a member of a college chess team and competing in Europe

2　Overcoming a handicap or barrier and learning or developing something that seemed out of reach, e.g. fear of water overcome so you could go on a sailing holiday

3   A personal achievement, e.g. looking after a young sibling when a parent was ill

4   Using negotiating or persuasive skills, e.g. taking part in a successful campaign to have the speed limit in the road lowered

5   Fund-raising, e.g. doing a parachute jump for charity

6   Getting a book or articles published in the local paper

7   Finishing the London Marathon

8   Coming second in a 'Best of Bands' competition

9   Part of a small team on a field trip that discovered a new species of insect

Some of these may not be appropriate for a CV or application form, but they should give you confidence that you have achievements to be proud of and you may be asked about personal achievements at an interview.

ACTIVITY 29

1   Look through the above questions and also think through your various experiences.

2   Identify as many achievements or successes that you can and list them.

3   Can you identify three or four that you could add to the education, work and leisure sections of your CV?

4   Do you have enough for a separate section?

Contributions to society

This is another area where you may find it easier to include the details under school, university or work sections. If important enough to merit its own section – for example, if you want to include raising money for charity, relevant work during a gap year, long-term voluntary work, church or community work etc. – treat it just like the other sections:

➤ Create your own heading

➤ State clearly where, what, when, why and how you made your contribution(s)

Extra sections

If there is something you want to tell an employer that doesn't fit any of the above categories or that you want to emphasize separately, create one or more sections of your own. These could include anything from a list of your publications to living abroad or achieving a lifetime's ambition such as sailing round the world, playing the Edinburgh Fringe or setting up your own company.

ACTIVITY 30

1 Is there anything else you would want to include in your CV that would not be covered by the headings suggested so far?

2 What would be the best heading for your extra section?

3 Write the section.

Formatting

On paper, the aim is to produce a clear, professional-looking word-processed CV that is easy to read and work through and will also come out clearly if scanned or photocopied. Ideally:

- Use simple, clear fonts (no more than two different ones) in different sizes. Text must be large enough to read comfortably, so usually size 11 and above. Experiment with standard font sizes and styles, e.g. sans serif (no extra little lines at the ends of letters) such as Arial, or serif such as Times New Roman

- Print onto good-quality white paper – remember it is going to be handled so it needs to feel pleasant and withstand some wear

- Have wide enough margins and white space round entries so that it looks attractive and not cramped, and make sure everything is correctly aligned

- Each section should be separated from the next with sub-headings in a slightly larger font size (change the font colour or emphasize with bold) and make your points stand out using bullets or numbering

- Try to avoid underlining or using table borders as the text won't be so easy to read – just use spaces and formatting intelligently

- Number pages and, if it looks right, include a header or footer with your name in it, to make sure pages don't get lost

- Post flat in an A4 envelope, which, in the UK, will require suitable 'large letter' stamps

- Don't staple pages together – the recruiter may want to photocopy them

(Note that if you still feel you have to spend money on a professional CV service, the company may suggest binding your CV and adding a cover sheet etc. This is really quite unnecessary.)

EXAMPLE

There are different ways you can arrange, format and emphasize the details on your CV using shading, bullet points and bold or italics. Here are two alternatives:

CAREER HISTORY
W. Blogs and Co., Engineering Firm, Hartlepool
Assistant Finance Officer
- Responsible for . . .
- Contributed towards . . .
- Managed . . .

W. H. Smith, Newsagent, Bristol
Sales Assistant
- Involved in . . .
- Created . . .

OR

CAREER HISTORY
2009–2011   W. Blogs and Co., Engineering Firm, Hartlepool
                    Assistant Finance Officer
- Responsible for . . .
- Contributed towards . . .
- Managed . . .

Key achievements
- Played a key role in . . .
- Personally responsible for . . .

2011–2012   W. H. Smith, Newsagent, Bristol
                    Sales Assistant

Sending

If you are posting your CV, there will usually be a covering letter in the envelope as well.

When sending a CV in the body of an email, you will obviously have few formatting options, but you can still add spaces, capitals etc. to separate sections.

If attaching your CV to an email or uploading it to the Web, use a version that has been saved in a standardized and easily recognized file format, e.g. Microsoft Word, PDF or Rich Text Format. (PDF is ideal if you don't want anything happening to the format or content.)

Don't forget to check that the CV is attached properly – there is nothing worse than having to send a second email apologizing for leaving it off!

APPLICATION FORMS

Much of the advice in the CVs section applies equally here, so read through the paragraphs above if you have not already done so.

Large employers in particular spend a great deal of time designing their application forms and they all believe that their wording and the order in which they put the questions is better than anyone else's. It is also, sadly, a means by which employers can force applicants to answer questions they would prefer to avoid, e.g. on their health record, why they left their previous jobs, their exact salary etc., so be prepared for a few nasty surprises.

One day we may reach the stage where you won't have to complete a separate form every time you apply to a different employer, but until then you will make life simpler for yourself if you keep all the facts and figures handy so that you can look things up quickly.

Keeping copies of your completed forms is very important. Obviously that is easy on a computer, but you may need to scan or photocopy finished forms if they are handwritten. Not only do you need to reread them before an interview but also, if you have written a good answer on one form and you are asked exactly the same question, you can copy your text into other forms to save time.

Basic rules

There are certain common sense rules to follow when completing forms:

1 Complete every box. If they say they won't accept CVs, make sure you don't write 'see CV' into every box. The only time this is acceptable is if, after completing most of a box, it is more sensible to refer to your CV because there are too many extra details (such as a large number of part-time jobs or string of qualifications) to fit in.

2 Follow every instruction. If asked to write in black ink, include a photograph, stick to a maximum number of words or attach other documents with a paper clip, make sure you do so.

3 Check the completed form very carefully. You will want your final version to be perfect – no unreadable handwriting, crossings out, spelling mistakes or grammatical errors, extra notes squeezed into the margins or overflowed space. It is hard to use a word processor for most forms so, unless you are offered an online version capable of being filled in on a computer, you will have to complete them manually. As space is limited, it can often be a good idea to make a copy and try out a draft version first, just to make sure you use each box fully and can get everything in.

4 Include key information. There are usually guidelines on what is essential and what is desirable in any advertisement. Make sure you include the facts somewhere that show you meet the criteria. If there really is no relevant question concerning one vital piece of information, find a more general box to put it in. (Application forms are generally seen as a combination of covering letter and

CV and so you won't usually write an accompanying letter in which you could have included these details.)

5 Meet the country's employment criteria. Application forms have a section concerning your ability to work in this country (or overseas if you are applying for a job abroad) and so you have to confirm your nationality or whether you have a valid work permit. It is important to answer this accurately.

6 Take care with extra pages. Very often, you will need to put extra information on a separate sheet. To make sure this doesn't get lost, add your name in a header or footer.

Completing the form

In the last Step, you were offered advice on how to analyse advertisements and identify areas where you could offer evidence that would support your application. What you must do on application forms is avoid answering any question with an empty statement, i.e. one where there is no evidence that what you say is true.

For example, if one of the requirements is to be computer literate, an empty statement would be: 'I am very good with computers.'

An evidence-based statement would be: 'I have a GCSE in IT and one of the modules in my degree course was on Cybercrime. This involved developing in-depth internet searching skills.'

ACTIVITY 31

This is a common application form question: 'Many jobs need a certain level of IT/computer proficiency for the job to be performed effectively. As part of your suitability for a job, please give details of your IT skills and experience.'

Attempt to answer this question as fully as possible.

To make sure you emphasize your suitability for the position, it is perfectly acceptable to introduce each section with a phrase that includes the employer's own trigger words. These will be found in their advertisements or job descriptions. But you must then go on to include the evidence for your beliefs or statements. So, by all means start by stating that you are a good team player, excellent communicator, manage time well, have leadership qualities etc., but then back that up with examples.

For the details about computer literacy, for example, you could perhaps phrase your full answer as follows:

I am very experienced with computers as I have been using them since I was nine. Following my A grade in IT at GCSE, I chose a computer-based Cybercrime module on my degree course, which involved developing in-depth internet search skills. I am an active member of Facebook and Twitter and have my own profile on LinkedIn. I also helped design the website for my father's building company and have some knowledge of JavaScript, coding, HTML and CSS.

Why do you want this job?

As you have already learned, the main questions in the mind of any employer are 'Can you do the job?' and 'Why do you want this type of work/this job/to work for us?' You will always have to have answers prepared for these two questions. If they are not framed clearly on a form and all you seem to be offered is a box in which to put 'any additional information', make sure you put the answers to these questions here.

You may find the wording of the question 'why do you want this job?' expressed in a complex way, so check each line carefully to make sure you have answered *every* part and don't miss anything out. (Although this and the 'What can you offer?' question are often combined on application forms, don't make a mistake and miss out the explanation for your motivation.)

EXAMPLE

The Kiln Group graduate application form offers the 'double' question in this format:

Please explain to us:
- What attracts you to the particular graduate scheme you are applying for
- Why you think you are suitable (this relates to what you have to offer)
- Your career choice
- How you plan to achieve your goals in relation to this

There are a number of different answers you might give to show motivation, depending on the work and your own background, and often you will need to give answers that take into account a combination of these. You will normally need to give reasons for applying for both the overall sector or type of work *and* that organization in particular. Here are a few approaches:

1 A strong and logical link made between your choice of degree subject and the employer or the career/job they are offering.
For example, you may be on an Ocean Science degree course and have been studying scuba diving in your spare time so that you could hunt for buried shipwrecks, and this company is one of the largest shipwreck surveyors offering work.

Or: During your final year you specialized in the genetics of plant breeding and decided to find work with a large seed company where you could continue to study and apply your knowledge.

145

2 A strong and logical link made between your past experience or interests, e.g. in a job or through your leisure or other activities and the career/job or employer. For example, you may love working with small children with evidence to show this, and have chosen to go into nursery or primary school teaching; or you may have developed an interest in housing, serving as a Hall representative and also working as a volunteer in the student union's accommodation office so now you are applying for work with a Housing Association or Property Management company.

3 A desire to enter a certain type of work because of your values. For example, if you value cherishing and looking after our heritage, you may want to go into furniture restoration, the world of antiques or to work for English Heritage or the National Trust.

4 A good reason to work for them in particular. For example, this could be related to:

   a Wanting to work in that particular industrial sector or with that type of product or service. For example, a fascination with and knowledge of trains leading to you applying for a place on a rail franchise training scheme, or wanting to use your languages in the political sphere and hoping to join the European Civil Service

   b Because of something the individual organization has done or is involved in that makes them particularly attractive, e.g. a large-scale project that is bringing great benefits, being the market leader in a new and developing sector etc.

   c The organization's values/aims. For example, wanting to join a retail organization where staff are all members or partners

   d Because the work fits in with the future role you want for yourself in society. For example, to help others you may want a job with an international or medical charity, or to earn a top salary and be involved in the business world, you may want a job as a management consultant

146

e   Because your background makes this particular post or scheme the most suitable. For example, you may already have some connection with them through work experience or a placement and you may want it to continue

f   The opportunities they offer their employees such as further qualifications, varied experience or international postings etc. For example, there are more opportunities if you have chartered status, and they offer training that will lead to membership of the relevant professional body

ACTIVITY 32

1   For any job you are or may be applying for, identify the key reason(s) for your choice.

2   Write out a paragraph that explains clearly why you have chosen that organization to apply to.

Each year, the *Guardian* produces a publication showing the top 300 most popular employers chosen by graduates. This does not mean they had large numbers of vacancies on offer, and so getting into organizations that attract so many applicants is particularly tough. You can see the data for 2012–13 at targetjobs.co.uk/uk300. The top twenty were:

1   Google
2   BBC TV
3   GSK – pharmaceutical company
4   NHS graduate training scheme
5   MI6
6   Channel 4
7   Innocent Drinks
8   Teaching
9   Goldman Sachs
10   Amnesty International
11   Oxfam
12   MI5
13   Foreign & Commonwealth Office
14   Rolls Royce
15   Civil Service fast stream

16 Pricewaterhousecoopers

17 Microsoft

18 Unilever

19 AstraZeneca – bio-
    pharmaceutical company

20 John Lewis

Whether it is the individual named organizations or the general business sectors that attract so many applicants is not clear. Certainly with only one retailer, one drinks company and one engineering company in the top twenty, it is likely that they top the list just because their brands are so well known.

Whatever the reasons, if you want to compete for jobs within these particular organizations you will ideally have relevant work experience (perhaps gained through a placement), possibly a relevant degree and be able to offer excellent educational qualifications. Once you can do that, you need to find a really good answer to the 'why I want to work for you' question.

ACTIVITY 33

1 Choose one of the top twenty most popular organizations listed above.

2 Try to identify two or three good reasons you could give for working for them.

3 If none of the named organizations appeal, think of a type of work (such as IT, marketing, accountancy, administration etc.) that interests you and that would be available within some of these organizations, and justify your choice of work but also the choice of employer. (If necessary, carry out some research into the named organizations first. It is quite likely that you will be applying to some organizations or to work in some sectors that you know little about, simply because they are the only ones offering opportunities in your chosen field. So this activity should be useful practice.)

What can you offer?

The wording of this question can vary quite a bit, e.g. 'why should we offer you the job?' or 'what makes you the most suitable candidate?' etc., but they all require the same answer. This part of the form is where you sell yourself as the ideal candidate. Make sure that somewhere in the answer you emphasize how you meet all their essential criteria and as many desirable ones as you can.

EXAMPLE

Sometimes, the question is phrased helpfully to give you clues as to exactly what to put. This typical example from the Met Office shows you what they will expect to read:

With reference to both the essential and desirable criteria listed in the job description, please state the extent to which you meet each of these criteria in turn as they are listed in the job description. Describe how your knowledge, skills and experience will enable you to perform this job well. In particular we are looking for evidence of key things you have achieved and how you went about making those achievements. Read the accompanying application form guidance prior to completing this section.

The example uses the word 'achievements', which can be hard to identify if you are a 'normal' graduate who hasn't done much outside university. Look at the examples on pages 136–7 for ideas of what to include and then tie these in with the job requirements.

ACTIVITY 34

1   Take one job you are applying for, check the job details carefully and then note down which examples you will need to provide to answer the question for yourself.

2   If necessary, go back to Step 4 and reread the sections on where and how to find evidence.

Competencies and STAR answers

Most open-ended questions are difficult to answer, and the hardest part of any application is usually where you have to provide evidence of transferable skills such as leadership qualities, integrity, flexibility, creativity etc., as listed on page 16.

Employers like simple, straightforward answers to questions and, when it comes to competencies, one acceptable business approach is the 'STAR' technique. This involves answering a question in four parts which, in the words of Transport for London's advice for graduates, are:

Situation – briefly describe the background to the situation

Task – specifically describe your responsibility

Action – describe what you did, but more importantly how you went about it [this is the most important section]

Result – describe the outcome of your actions

(Of course, in your answer, don't use these four actual words as paragraph headings.)

Taking a specific example, if you want to provide evidence of initiative, here is an answer using the STAR approach:

Situation: 'I am interested in medieval history and got involved in longbow-making first of all by making the leather scabbard for a sword. I then moved on to making arrows and, after reading a few books, started making a yew longbow.'

Task: 'I wanted to learn more advanced skills and also how to handle the tools better, so I looked on the internet for a teacher.'

Action: 'I discovered someone living quite near and contacted him so that we could arrange a couple of hours' training. It was going so well that I wanted to continue, as well as join in the competitive shooting he organized, but didn't have enough money. So I suggested I pay him by giving him guitar lessons.'

Result: 'I am now getting good at longbow shooting, have made a couple of successful bows and really enjoy my new hobby.'

ACTIVITY 35

1   Look at the list of transferable skills/traits on page 16 or identify one key skill you will need to display.
2   Use the STAR technique to describe a situation where you displayed the skill or personal trait.

Sections related to work

These are very often set out in table form, and in these cases you will have to comply with their headings. Usually, when you describe your work experience, you will include:

➢ Name of the organization and type of business

➢ Dates you worked for them

➢ Your job title or role

➤ Your main responsibilities

➤ Any achievements

Dates: Unless the heading specifies dates more exactly, it should be good enough either to put month and year, or even just years if it was over an extended period. This way the odd short gaps in time, which are not really relevant anyway, will not be highlighted. For example: 'Pizza restaurant – part-time waiter (2005–2008)'

Content: As always, you will want to stress your role, responsibilities, skills, achievements and any other selling points you can think of. The section on CVs covers this approach in some depth.

Interests

Try to put down interests that will add to what you can offer. Unlike on a CV, you may not be able to avoid this section, but fortunately everyone has some interests, and even the most mundane such as cooking, gardening or reading science fiction can be written up in an amusing or interesting way or show off a few transferable skills.

EXAMPLE

Cooking – I never cooked before going to university but I have enjoyed teaching myself, particularly how to make curries, and find it has improved my social life as well as budgeting skills. In my final year, I set up a cookery society and members regularly run a version of *Come Dine with Me*.

Additional information

This is the place to warn them of any plans you have to be away or if there are any special circumstances they need to be aware of. You may also want to put in here anything positive that there was no suitable place for elsewhere.

It is the one section you can leave blank if there is nothing to add.

ONLINE APPLICATIONS

These are likely to ask just the same questions as paper forms, but you have to bear in mind that:

1 Once you submit the form, you will not have a chance to make any changes.

2 Application forms don't usually have built in spelling or grammar checkers so you do need to take particular care. Ideally, open up a word-processing program and draft out the answers to any questions first. You can then edit and spell-check them before copying and pasting them into the form. This process is useful for three other reasons:

   a You may not be able to save a copy of your completed application form. As you should always keep a copy of anything you write – for example, to read through before an interview – save these draft answers under the name of the employer and date you sent off the application.

   b If the computer crashes halfway through, you will have copies of everything you have written so far.

   c If you are given a word count limit, using your word processor will allow you to check and edit your text to meet their requirements.

3 You may have to take a psychometric test as part of the application

process, so see 'Step 6 – Going for Interviews' for advice on what to expect.

REFEREES

References are statements made in your support, often to vouch for your character as well as work or academic record. (The individuals making the statements are your referees and the statements themselves are the references.)

Things have changed now and referees can no longer get away with rude or negative comments safe in the knowledge that you will never know about them. This means that references have become quite bland. You can ask to read any reference and challenge them if necessary, but you should still try to choose someone who will be positive about you.

You will need to provide the names and contact details of two or three people who can vouch for you in terms of:

➢ Being who you say you are

➢ Achieving what you say you achieved

➢ Pointing out things the employer needs to know about you

➢ If you have the choice, select the person who is most relevant to the job you are applying for

You would normally provide details of a university academic such as your Head of Department, supervisor or personal tutor as your main referee, to confirm that your degree results or expected outcomes are accurate. Then you need to find at least one other person such as a line manager at work. If you have no work or volunteer experience, find an individual of some standing in the community who knows you quite well, such as a doctor, lawyer, family friend or past school or college teacher, or someone you know officially through other activities, e.g. a sports coach, choir master or church leader. If you are stuck for a name or need a third reference, use a second academic, but try to find someone who is in a different field or knows you in a different way to the first one.

As well as full name, title and contact details including email address and phone numbers, put down the relationship you have to the referee, e.g. state if they are a previous employer or tutor etc.

EXAMPLE

Mrs Diane Rowbottom
Head of Biochemical Laboratory
Sterrpoint Pharmaceuticals
Harlow Road
Oxford, OX1 2ER
Tel: 01865 3445222
d.rowbottom@sterrpoint.com
(Industrial placement supervisor during my year out at
Warwick University)

Your referees are hopefully going to boost your chances of getting a job and the more they know the better. Make sure you send them full details of the jobs you are applying for, if necessary send them your CV or a completed application form and ask their permission, including if you may carry on using them until you are offered employment. If you haven't spoken to them for a while, you may want to update them on anything relevant that has been happening to you.

If applying from within a job and not wanting to advertise that you are looking elsewhere, don't include referees' details unless they are required. In this case, put down somewhere that you do not want them approached in advance of an interview or job offer.

Whether or not you get the job, it is polite to let your referees know the outcome and thank them for their support.

ACTIVITY 36

1   Identify two or three suitable referees.

2   Collect together all their details.

3   Sound them out early about using them for your job applications.

STAYING MOTIVATED

You may live in a part of the country where work is particularly hard to find and, even if you are making applications in London or other apparently affluent areas, it could still take a long while to find a job.

Keeping motivated is important but very difficult, especially when, despite doing everything you feel is right, you are still getting rejected or not even having your applications acknowledged.

It may help if instead of viewing job hunting as a single large, intractable problem, you break it down into a number of small, manageable steps. Think about your situation and decide on an overriding issue you could tackle. For example,:

If you are feeling hopeless, isolated or depressed about the whole process:

➤ Is there a counsellor, or careers adviser you haven't seen for a while, whom you could go and talk to?

➤ Is there an online forum such as www.thestudentroom.co.uk you could join where you could communicate with other people who might be in your situation?

➤ Is there a networking group such as Round Table or Ladies Circle in your area that you could join?

If you believe you could do the jobs you are applying for but are not getting offered any interviews:

➤ Is there someone who could look through your applications and give advice on ways they could be improved?

➤ Is it worth spending money getting a professional CV drawn up, to see if that makes any difference?

➤ If you can see weak areas, can you do anything to strengthen what you have to offer?

Or if there are simply no paid jobs in the area:

➤ Could you get a book out of the library to help you work on a gap in your skills or knowledge base?

➤ Can you find a place to volunteer such as a charity shop, old people's home or hospital where you would enjoy working?

➤ Are there any local employers who could provide unpaid work experience or shadowing so that you could develop useful contacts and relevant skills?

EXAMPLE

Many graduates worry about losing benefits if they do unpaid work. According to the Department of Work and Pensions, they 'know that volunteering can give you a much better chance of finding paid work. So you can volunteer as many hours as you like while you're getting benefits as long as you keep to the rules for getting them, i.e. if you get Jobseeker's Allowance, you will still need to be looking for paid work. You must be free to go to an interview if given forty-eight hours' notice and you must be able to start work within one week of them giving you notice. You must not be paid money or anything else for volunteering. It's OK to be paid your expenses but you must tell them what you get. So make sure you can keep your receipts. You must contact Jobcentre Plus if you want to do any volunteering and they will ask you to fill in a simple form telling them about the volunteering you want to do'.

Goal setting

Whatever issue you identify, the manageable approach is to set a series of SMART goals. This means that you should aim to take one step at a time that is:

➢ Specific

➢ Measurable

➢ Attainable

➢ Realistic

➢ Time-limited

If we apply this approach to finding a voluntary position:

1 Decide on a Specific hospital, charity shop or nursery to contact.

2 Spend the Measurable time of half a day finding the full contact details for the right person and writing to or phoning them.

3 Make the voluntary position Attainable by being flexible about the amount of time or days on which you can work for them.

4 Understand they might need to check up on you or take up references so be Realistic about how long it might take to sort out.

5 Set a Time-limit, such as two weeks, by which you will have fixed up what seems a definite voluntary position or contacted them to check on progress.

When you reach your deadline, evaluate the goal. If it has been achieved, build on it at some future time to set yourself another goal. If not, revisit it, e.g. contact a different organization in the same way or apply the knowledge you have gained during this process to approach the problem slightly differently.

You may think acronyms like SMART are mumbo-jumbo business-speak, but breaking down a task into manageable steps and taking them one at a time can actually work and will certainly give you sense of achievement as each goal is reached.

No acknowledgements

Sadly, with the numbers of applicants applying for each job at the moment, some employers are so inundated that they may decide not even to acknowledge receiving your application.

You and I know that this is rude and, considering how much time they make you spend filling in forms and writing letters, it shouldn't happen. However, the key thing is to make sure your application was received and they have your contact details, and then get on with your life.

1   Double check your documentation to make sure you have included your current postal address, email address and a contact phone number.

2   If you are really worried about the mail, or for a crucial application, include a stamped self-addressed postcard that they can fill in to acknowledge your application was received (although even then, there is no guarantee they will take the time to complete and return it to you!).

3   Ideally a day or two before the deadline, phone the organization just to check your application was received. You should have time to send it in again if the worst has happened.

4   Keep a record of all applications and closing dates. If you make a large number of applications, it may be important to be able to check if you have applied to a particular organization before, and when the deadlines have passed.

5   Never sit and wait for an interview. Always keep working/studying/volunteering and applying elsewhere at the same time so you always have something in the pipeline.

SUMMARY

1   Use every means to find out about vacancies as many jobs are never advertised.

2   Networking is becoming one of the key methods for graduates to find work.

3   If you can get on an internship, your prospects are improved immensely as employers often take their employees from such schemes.

4   Make speculative applications as it can be very successful.

5   Always write a well-argued covering letter to go with your CV as it is the first document likely to be read by recruiters.

6   Prepare your CV carefully and make sure it is tailored to each vacancy.

7   However a CV is laid out, stress your personal qualities and key skills early in the document to show you meet their requirements.

8   Work on the achievements section as this will also come up in interviews.

9   Application forms must always address two fundamental questions: what you can offer and why you want the job.

10 Use various techniques to stay motivated as finding work can take time.

STEP 6

GOING FOR INTERVIEWS

Sadly, many people look wonderful on paper and turn out to be completely impossible in the flesh. The main purpose of an interview is to find out whether you are who you say you are and that you have all the qualities and potential you seem to have on paper. It is also a chance for applicants who were on the borderline to shine, or to use their persuasive skills to end up with a job offer.

As always, employers will want to make sure that:

➢ You can do the work

➢ You want to do the work

➢ You will fit in

An interview really should be a two-way process and you will have your own agenda too. You will need to make sure you find out enough information to make the right decision. For example, you may well decide after hearing about the job that you are no longer interested in the work on offer, or want to work for this particular organization.

INITIAL INTERVIEW

Depending on the level of the post you have applied for, as well as the size of the organization, you may be offered a single interview or have to go through a series of interviews and tests. If they organize second interviews and assessment centres, you may find that the initial interview is quite brief. No matter what type you think you will face, be fully prepared for a long, in-depth interview at all times.

A first interview may either take place on campus or at the organization's offices or workplace. Usually it will be one-to-one, but if it is the only interview they will conduct, you may find yourself talking to both a recruiter or someone from personnel and another member of staff such as a specialist, there to check your in-depth subject knowledge, or the person you will be working directly for.

For some organizations, there will be a panel interview – four or more different people will be gathered together and will usually have agreed in advance which different areas to cover, so that you will talk to each one in turn.

Planning your answers

The two questions you must be able to answer at an interview are: why you want this type of work, or to join this sector or named organization, and what you can offer. You also need to have some idea of where you might be going – either within their organisation or building on the skills, experience and responsibilities you will gain.

If you carried out a full analysis of the job you applied for, and provided evidence in your application of how you acquired the relevant skills and experience, reading through that documentation will be one of the best ways to prepare. At some time during the interview, they are likely to ask you to expand on what you put down and so you need to remind yourself about the examples you used to show them your capabilities, and be prepared to go into more detail.

Think 'scenarios' and remember the STAR approach (explained on page 150). In particular, think about examples you can offer where you used transferable skills like initiative, problem-solving, leadership, teamwork, planning and organizing, decision-making, communicating and persuasive skills. These are not topics that pop straight into your head so you do need to spend time preparing and remembering your examples. They will then sound fluent when you talk about them in the interview.

ACTIVITY 37

1 Choose four of the transferable skills or personal qualities listed above or on page 16.

2 Identify the best example you can find for each one, showing evidence that you have that skill or personal quality.

3 Set out the details in the form of a scenario or story.

4 Keep notes of these examples so you can refer to them before any interviews.

EXAMPLE

Here is one four-step approach to the transferable skill of problem-solving when asked to 'give an example of how you have used problem-solving skills':

1 Identify a problem you had

2 What were your options and the difficulty with each one?

3 What action did you take to solve the problem?

4 What was the outcome?

- **Problem** – in charge of organizing an event with an outside speaker, and learning the day before that they were ill.

- **Options** – cancel or postpone the event (difficult getting in touch with people in time), find an alternative speaker (where from?), put on a different event (what, and how to do this at short notice?)

- **Action** – discussed it with the committee and two members were willing to run a different session so we could have the speaker back later in the year

- **Outcome** – a very enjoyable and successful evening

As well as researching 'yourself', the more facts and figures about the recruiting organization that you have, the more you will impress them that you are serious about the job and the opportunities they are offering. As well as reading through the literature you have accumulated on them, keep up to date with relevant news or developments through the trade press and their own website so that you can talk about current issues.

ACTIVITY 38

1 Visit the website of one organization you hope to have an interview with.

2 Read what you can about them, their staff, their organization, their plans etc.

3 Identify one or two issues that might be raised at the interview or that you could ask a question about.

Here are a few examples of areas you might choose to research:

1 **Ernst & Young** (accountancy firm) sponsor the ITEM Club and their website provided a pre-Budget report on the UK economy in March 2013

2 **B & Q** (DIY retailer) have a number of policies related to ethics and the environment.

3 **The Co-operative Group** (food, finance and funeral services) now has a licence to offer legal services to the public.

4 **Saatchi & Saatchi** (advertising agency) carried out research into attitudes towards the UK high street after interviewing 11 million sixteen/twenty-nine-year-olds, and produced a downloadable report on their findings.

Typical questions

It is hard to guess what you might need to prepare for, but here are ten examples of typical questions you are likely to be asked at an interview. They are not difficult as long as you prepare your answers in advance. Think about what is behind the question, as that will influence your answer.

1 Tell me a little about yourself

What they will expect: That the information will show you in a positive light (emphasize initiative, honesty, hard-working etc.), will be relevant to the job and will be concise. You can include a small amount of personal or family information if it is important to show who you are, but keep it very brief and always emphasize your degree and relevant work or leisure choices.

What they don't want: Long, rambling answers that show you cannot keep your mind on the task (selling yourself at an interview), that are embarrassingly personal, completely irrelevant, boastful or go back too far into your past.

EXAMPLE

I am the first member of my family to go to university. I chose to study History and Archaeology because I was fascinated by the *Time Team* programmes on television, but didn't want to study archaeology exclusively. I chose a module on the Second World War and that made me decide I wanted to work with archives and living history in a war museum or similar environment. I needed to learn German to help with my studies so I joined an international pen-pal website and ended up spending six months staying with a friend in Munich.

---

2 What made you pick this job?

What they will expect: This is one of the two key questions you will have had to prepare already and so you should have all the answers at your fingertips. You could emphasize using particular skills, using your degree or past experience, the relationship of the work to one of your interests, how the role or organization would tie in with your values, or any previous links with the company. In an interview, it is fine to mention things like family connections (e.g. parents 'also' teachers or pharmacists etc.) or someone important in your life who introduced you to the career.

If possible, come up with a special reason for picking them, e.g. their size, their position in the market, particular customers or clients, their work in the community etc.

What they don't want: Evidence that you have no idea what the work entails, a very poor reason for your choice (e.g. all the various perks) or that it is clearly a second-best option.

3 Why should we employ you?

What they will expect: This is the second key question you should be well prepared for and should be based on their job description and basic requirements. Stress your relevant skills, experience, personal qualities, work knowledge, motivation and what you can bring to the job. Talk up all your best qualities and strengths, as long as you can back them up with examples.

What they don't want: To learn you don't have a good answer and can't talk about yourself in a way that makes you an attractive candidate.

4 What are your major strengths or weaknesses?

What they will expect: Strengths are the key skills and traits that you will have already put down on your CV or application forms, so choose the most important and relevant ones to talk about and provide evidence for.

With weaknesses, the key is to select one or two that are not going to be seen as serious failings (like dishonesty or laziness). Pick things that you do not do very well but that you have identified and are working on. (The question may be phrased slightly differently, e.g. what would your friends or colleagues say is your major weakness, but don't fall into the trap of identifying more negative traits.) If you can, think of a story you can tell where you explain a weakness and how you are overcoming it.

What they don't want: Serious character weaknesses, or a fault that will make you a poor employee.

EXAMPLE

I am quite shy and when I first started my degree I found it difficult to relax and talk to strangers at social gatherings. I am getting better now because I practise the trick of turning the conversation back onto other people and asking about them – once they start talking about themselves I no longer feel I have to perform or entertain them.

---

5 **Tell me how you dealt with a difficult experience at university or work?**
What they will expect: To learn how you deal with issues like confrontations, minor disasters or blunders and what you have learned from them.

What they don't want: 'I can't think of any', one that shows you didn't handle a situation well, or indicates that you didn't learn anything from it. In particular, never blame other people for being difficult to work with.

EXAMPLE

Four of us were meant to be producing a joint report, but one person didn't do any work and didn't show up for a couple of sessions. I went to find him and ask him why and he said he was bored with the direction we were taking. I suggested he tell everyone and put forward his own ideas, so we all sat down and talked it through and it was agreed to make some changes. He was then much keener and we worked well as a team.

---

6 **Where do you see yourself in five years' time?**

What they will expect: An answer that shows you have done your research and understand what they can offer. Your plans should tie in with the sort of career progression you could expect and show you are ambitious but realistic.

What they don't want: To find you have no plans or don't seem to understand the type of work you are entering or that you are unrealistic or far too ambitious.

EXAMPLE

This training scheme is for two years, and so at the end of it I hope to have decided which area to specialize in and then perhaps become qualified with chartered status. Eventually I would like to head up one of the branches in the north-east.

---

7 **What do you know about our business?**

What they will expect: To see how much research you have

carried out into their sector or company, whether your knowledge is superficial or out of date or if you have any ideas to contribute about developments in their field.

What they don't want: To discover you know nothing about them, have not tried to find out and may even be misinformed.

8 What have been your major achievements?

What they will expect: Having identified a range of achievements when preparing your CV or application forms (see pages 136–7 for suggestions), you should be able to draw on one or two that emphasize your work-related or transferable skills or that show you have excelled at something in your life, overcome an obstacle or made a major contribution. Ideally, don't go too far back in time.

What they don't want: To hear that you have none, or for you to pick something that would not be viewed as much of an achievement.

9 What do you do in your spare time?

What they will expect: You will have already covered this in your self-analysis, so select one or two activities that are particularly interesting or unusual, or that show you in the best possible light.

What they don't want: To hear that you have none, or that your interests are superficial (drinking etc.) or show you in a poor light, e.g. only pursuing passive hobbies like TV and listening to music, or just going along with the crowd.

10 What other jobs have you applied for?

What they will expect: Make sure you mention one or two that have a logical relationship to this particular application or to your degree or past experience.

What they don't want: One or more jobs that seem to have no bearing on your reasons for applying to them, or show you haven't made any serious career decisions. They also won't be interested in superficial reasons for choices you have made.

EXAMPLE

I really want to start on a graduate training scheme like yours and make my career in this area, so I have applied to a couple of other large retailers offering opportunities in the south-west. If I don't get on any of these schemes, I have also put my name down for a one-year retailing internship as I felt the experience would be invaluable if I had to apply again next year for a full-time position.

PREPARING

Everyone gets nervous before an interview, so expect to feel ill, anxious or tense. As long as you have read through all your notes and examples and give yourself lots of time on the day to get there and settle, all you can do is try to stay calm, listen to the questions carefully and respond in as natural and positive a way as you can.

Affirmations

If you get particularly stressed at the thought of an in interview, an approach in which Paul McKenna (author of *Change Your Life in 7 Days* and *Instant Confidence*) is a great believer is 'affirmations'. These are honest and realistic statements (or 'positive self-talk') spoken out loud that, when repeated, either become self-fulfilling or at least can help overcome negative thoughts and feelings.

We all know that a poor self-image feeds on itself, so in the same way a strong self-belief can become ingrained and help you stay motivated and feel more confident. If you tell yourself repeatedly that you can succeed in something like job-hunting or interviews, then many psychologists and counsellors believe that you have a better chance of doing so.

To test if it works for you:

1　Write out a positive statement, expressed in the present tense that starts with 'I'. For example: 'I am just the right candidate for this job' or 'I am a confident and enthusiastic person'.
2　Repeat it out loud as often as you can, especially when you start feeling negative about your situation.
3　Write it down on a card or pin it where you will see it, to remind yourself of the sentiment.
4　Try it for a few weeks to give it a chance to work and repeat it before any stressful situation like an interview.

Before the interview

Unless you are sure that the organization welcomes unconventional dress or an informal approach, it is best to err on the safe side:

■　Make an effort with your appearance. Have clean shoes, tidy hair, take off mouth or nose rings etc. and go for a sombre suit or jacket and trousers for men and neat skirt and jacket for women. Sadly, some people have a prejudice against beards so decide if you want to shave or not, and cut back on perfume and jewellery.

■　Take as little as possible with you. You may be able to leave your coat, umbrella and a briefcase at reception but if not, you won't want to take anything too bulky in with you – so don't go shopping first!

■　Unless asked to provide degree certificates, legal documents or a portfolio, you usually don't take any documents in with you. If you really have to, you could possibly take in a notebook, but it is not conventional practice. It could even be a distraction, as looking down to find information may mean you miss body language clues and facial expressions.

- Get there early. Make sure you are clear how to get to the venue, give yourself plenty of travelling time and keep a contact telephone number handy in case you are delayed. They are likely to be able to rearrange interviews if they get enough notice.

In the interview room

When you walk into the room, only shake hands if someone clearly presents their hand to you. Otherwise, it can become rather awkward, especially if there are several people present.

If you are offered a cup of coffee or tea, my personal advice would be to say no. It can be quite hard juggling a hot cup and being interviewed at the same time, and even worse if you happen to spill it.

Obviously, if there is only one interviewer you will keep good eye contact at all times. It is more difficult if faced with two or three people or a large number around a table. In this case, the best approach is to concentrate on speaking directly to the person who puts the question. Now and again try to take in everyone else with your reply as you will appear more warm and friendly, but keep your eye-sweep brief and come back to the individual you are addressing to check that they are satisfied with your answer.

When the interview comes to an end, keep things simple. Thank them for seeing you and then leave. Again, don't feel you have to shake anyone's hand unless the interviewer(s) make the approach.

QUESTIONS TO ASK THEM

It is really important to have one or two questions to ask at the end. If you follow up something that has cropped up in the interview, it shows you were paying attention; if you ask more about the work or the organization, it shows motivation and that you have taken your research seriously; if you ask about using a relevant special skill you have, it might add to what you can offer; and it may be your only chance to get a full answer to a genuine concern before you have to decide whether to accept a job offer or not.

Take great care not to ask a prepared question that they have actually answered during the interview, unless you need 'further details'.

Here are the sorts of areas your questions can cover:

➤ More about the job or scheme you are applying for, e.g. what will happen during your first few months

➤ Clarification concerning your initial training, gaining qualifications, timescales or locations you might work at

➤ Further information about your future – career prospects and promotion

➤ Opportunities to use or develop skills such as languages, computing, writing, training or supervising

➤ The criteria for assessment and measuring performance

➤ Future plans for the organization – growth, new markets, downsizing etc.

➤ Follow up on any special information you discovered about them during your research

You may also want to ask when you will hear the results of the interview.

ACTIVITY 39

1   Think about an organization you expect an interview with.

2   Note down three different questions you might ask at the end of an interview. Ideally, find things that there isn't much information about in their literature or online.

TELEPHONE INTERVIEWS

For many jobs that involve telephone use, or where employers receive too many applications for a single job, they may start with a chat on the telephone. This could be to establish the time and place for an actual interview, to help eliminate no-hopers or will be a full first interview. It is a useful way for them to narrow down the field if you give poor, inarticulate answers, and they can also check that you have reasonable telephone skills. Usually, you will still end up with a final face-to-face interview but that may be after they have concluded the job is probably yours.

Here are five tips for telephone interviews:

- Give yourself time to prepare. If they ring out of the blue and expect to talk to you there and then, make it clear you are not free and organize a set time and date when you know you can talk freely and quietly without interruption. You will then be able to prepare in exactly the same way that you would do for any other interview.

- Have your CV or application form and other background notes plus pencils and paper ready. You may have time to look up information (and, even if not, it may give you extra confidence) and can also make notes during the discussion.

- Take care to provide concise answers as there will be no eye contact and you won't be able to pick up body-language clues, e.g. if you are boring or irritating them. Listen extra hard and ask for clarification to make sure you understand the questions, and check back occasionally to see how much detail they are expecting or if they need any more.

- Take your time, but speak at a normal speed – neither gabbling nor speaking really slowly. Don't let them fluster or intimidate you, especially if you aren't that comfortable on the telephone. They may be taking notes anyway, so small gaps between questions and answers are fine.

▪ Try to sound enthusiastic, warm and friendly and thank them for the opportunity to talk to them.

At the end, make sure you get their full details (if they haven't contacted you in writing in advance), so that you can get in touch in the future.

Telephoning for further information

For some posts, you may be told in the advertisement to contact a particular member of staff for further information. In a sense, this can turn out to be a type of interview as that person may well be your eventual interviewer or line manager or be involved in the selection of candidates to invite for an interview.

Do your preparation work first so that you sound intelligent and knowledgeable and ask sensible questions. Only raise concerns if they won't make you appear a weak candidate, and be friendly and enthusiastic at all times. Every member of staff, no matter at what level they work, deserves politeness and respect.

FOLLOW UP

There are two main reasons why you should not forget all about an interview once it is over:

➢ If you are called back for a second interview, there may be things you said or questions you were asked that need to be researched further

➢ If you are turned down, reflecting on what took place will usually help you identify weaknesses or areas where you could prepare better or make improvements before the next interview

If you are rejected and they don't tell you why, try to get the interviewer to give you some feedback. Hopefully you will have the name and position of the individual concerned, but even just the date, location and job you applied for should mean the organization can trace them for you. Then you can write or telephone and ask for pointers on how you could improve your performance in future interviews.

Don't just ask 'why wasn't I selected?' or you could leave yourself open to the unhelpful comment that there were too many other candidates who were better qualified.

Saying thank you

People worry about whether they should do more than say 'thank you' as they leave the interview room. There are no rules, but common sense seems to suggest:

➤ It should be enough if you are clearly one of a large number of applicants being interviewed for a 'standard' job

➤ It is a good idea to write a very brief thank you note to anyone who arranged to see you specially, and in it you could emphasize your continued enthusiasm for the post

ASSESSMENT CENTRES

It is very common for candidates applying for high-level positions, including those on graduate training schemes, to be asked to attend not only a first interview but also a more extended second or multi-assessment event. This will usually take place at head office, a hotel or a training establishment and will consist of tests and group exercises as well as further interviews. The process can last for several hours or even one to two days, and during that time you will be observed and your behaviour and interactions with others, as well as your test and interview results, taken into account.

Everyone understands that this is a stressful event, but being invited to an assessment centre means you are a strong potential candidate with a good chance of receiving a job offer, as long as you don't go off the rails or fail all the tests.

Exercises and tests

Here are the most common activities that can take place at an assessment centre apart from the usual one-to-one or panel interviews:

➤ In-tray exercise

➤ Case study

➤ Group discussion

➤ Role play

➤ Teamwork exercise

➤ Presentation

➤ Psychometric tests (see page 181)

In all cases, read through the instructions and follow them carefully. If, for example, you need to write a report or set high or low priorities on items, give yourself time to complete all the tasks so that you get maximum marks.

In-tray exercise
Typically, you will be given a variety of telephone messages, emails, letters, faxes and reports and asked to prioritize them and then show how you would handle each one as well as justify your decisions. Actions could include writing brief notes and delegating tasks to an assistant as well as working on items yourself. There may be time to actually summarize reports or draft replies to messages during the exercise. It is likely that one or two new tasks will arrive during the session as the exercise is trying to simulate a real-life office environment.

It is worth reading through everything quickly first, to see if some items are related. If, say, decisions about one letter affect the answer you give to an email or the conclusion in a report you need to write, it is important to pick that up before getting into the details of the task.

Case study

Case-study exercises are normally carried out in groups so your interaction with others will also be assessed, but you may be given a problem to analyse and asked to work on your own. Commonly, you will be presented with a scenario setting out a business problem and will be given supporting facts and figures. You will need to evaluate the situation, interpret the data, consider alternative strategies and use the factual information to come up with a recommendation for what you regard as the best solution. This will then have to be conveyed to the assessors as a written or verbal report or you may be asked questions about it. If you are preparing a written report, use subheadings and other techniques to set out your arguments as clearly and logically as possible.

Group discussion

The group may be given a single topic or a range of topics to discuss, usually within a set time and you may have to act a role such as chairperson, secretary or timekeeper. Your aim should be to make your presence felt, but always in a polite and considerate way (never make derogatory remarks about anyone else's comments), making good points and taking the group with you, but also acknowledging the contributions made by others. Your aim should be to help get the group as a whole to reach its goal. If the discussion is getting sidetracked or bogged down, the ideal would be for you to find a way to move it forward. Whatever happens, never forget you are being assessed; take care that you don't get carried away just because you have strong personal feelings on a particular issue.

Role play

You may be assigned a role such as that of a manager or assistant and be asked to show how you would deal with a difficult situation.

The other role may be played by one of the assessors or members of the organization. Alternatively, they may get in actors briefed in the role. The only advice is to use your common sense and behave as you would expect someone in your position to behave – politely, firmly and fairly, while staying assertive. Try not to make promises or offer something you could not deliver, but your aim should be to reach a satisfactory conclusion for both you and your opposite number.

Teamwork exercise

Here, it is your interaction with others that is the key, and only groups that cooperate are likely to be successful. So you may have to build or construct something using plastic tubes, paper and glue, bricks etc., play a game, do a puzzle or create something after first gathering further information. You may have to interpret written instructions and assign individual roles so that you can carry out the task as quickly and efficiently as possible. Sometimes the exercise will be more like a multi-discussion or case-study exercise where, for example, one group has to negotiate for limited resources against the other groups.

Presentation

Whether this is an individual or group presentation, it is important to plan and structure what you are going to say so that you present all the key points in a logical fashion. Try not to rely too much on technological aids, keep good eye contact with the audience, exhibit confident body language, speak clearly and keep within any time limit. It is usually a good idea in any talk or speech to introduce what you are going to say and end clearly with a summary of your main points, a final conclusion or an idea for your audience to take away.

What they are looking for

Apart from further straightforward and panel interviews where the interviewers will be checking your knowledge, experience and motivation, the variety of tests and situations will help the assessors identify other things about you such as your:

1 Behaviour in a group. During group discussions or physical teamwork exercises, the ideal candidate will show initiative, leadership, good listening skills, cooperation, that they can get on with others, persuasive skills and the ability to put forward cogent arguments. Negative traits, like talking too much, not listening to others or not following instructions, being too shy to say anything or deferring easily to other people's ideas, will all be noted.

2 Communication skills. Whether giving an actual talk or summarizing your conclusions following a case study or group discussion exercise, these will all test your speaking ability, the way you present an argument, your persuasive skills, your ability to make jargon or technical terms understandable to a lay audience, your ability to use presentation aids and if you can think on your feet (for example, if you have had little warning of the subject matter or need to take questions).

3 Positive test results after taking ability, reasoning or personality tests (see the section on Psychometric Tests below).

4 Business sense. Many of the exercises such as working through an in-tray of tasks, discussing case studies or taking part in role play will show how much you understand and are able to analyse situations, solve problems, make decisions and come to sensible conclusions. In-tray exercises also test your ability to prioritize, read for meaning and your time-management skills, as you have to work speedily and accurately through a number of tasks.

5 Personal qualities. Your behaviour will be monitored not only during group activities but also when you are socializing with others at all levels or even relaxing between sessions. They will note whether you are punctual, friendly, enthusiastic and polite, whether you stay in control of your emotions and if you can handle stress.

PSYCHOMETRIC TESTS

No recruitment process can be foolproof and many employers like to have a wide range of indicators on candidates, particularly those that seem to provide an objective measure. Tests may also help them screen out a large number of unsuitable candidates quickly and cheaply if they have too many applicants to deal with comfortably.

Personality questionnaires and numerical, verbal, logical and other types of ability or reasoning tests, such as those for spatial awareness, clerical or mechanical skills, have been around a long time and for many specialist or graduate-level jobs you are likely to be asked to complete one or even a battery of different tests.

Although it is hard to change your personality, you may be able to improve your ability and reasoning scores by practising similar tests, taking part in quizzes and doing crosswords and puzzles, as well as brushing up on your mental arithmetic.

Personality questionnaires

There cannot be a 'correct' personality for a job, but employers may have two concerns: whether you have any extreme personality traits that might make you an unsuitable or unmanageable candidate, or if you have the appropriate balance of traits and temperament when compared to successful members of staff doing the job you are applying for. For example, if they believe they need an outgoing, lively, sociable person for the position and your results indicate you are shy, introverted and prefer your own company, they will probably want to explore the results during an interview.

Many of the tests developed by occupational psychologists are based around five work-related personality traits drawn along a scale from:

1 Extrovert–Introvert
2 Confident–Sensitive
3 Attention to detail–Unstructured
4 Tough-minded–Agreeable
5 Conforming–Creative

To score particularly highly at either end of each scale, candidates would be likely to display particular behaviours which the personality tests are meant to identify. For example:

➢ Extroverts are likely to be more talkative, enthusiastic, persuasive and gregarious

➢ Introverts are more reserved and shy, inhibited, not natural communicators

➢ Tough-minded people are not good team players, but are goal-orientated and able to make unpopular decisions

➢ Agreeable people are empathetic, tolerant, patient and democratic

Some psychologists have gone on to analyse certain work roles in terms of these traits so that if you are supportive, sociable, flexible, adaptable, perceptive, a good listener, have a calming influence and are a mediator, you are seen to make a good team member. If you are innovative, inventive, creative, original, imaginative, unorthodox and problem-solving, you are more likely to be a creative element in an organization.

The common types of questions you might face in one of these tests include:

➢ True or false questions, e.g. 'I find routine boring'

➤ Alternatives, e.g. do you see yourself as thick-skinned or thin-skinned?

➤ Being asked to rate your own behaviours, e.g. would you say you are an extremely good, good, neither good nor bad, poor or extremely poor listener

➤ Selecting the most appropriate or accurate out of four unrelated descriptions of your behavior, e.g. a) enjoy organizing events, b) sometimes get angry, c) are talkative, d) resolve conflicts at work. Over the course of the test, your personality and the consistency of your answers will both be picked up.

EXAMPLE

On a Tesco application form, applicants were asked to pick the least and most fitting descriptions of themselves out of four statements, such as:

I am the sort of person who:

A) Gives support to other people . . .
B) Negotiates with others . . .
C) Is able to problem solve . . .
D) Speaks clearly . . .

I am the sort of person who:

A) Changes people's views . . .
B) Treats others in fair and consistent ways . . .
C) Works with others to achieve group objectives . . .
D) Checks all details . . .

CONTINUED

I am the sort of person who:

A) Shares knowledge with others . . .
B) Is effective in leading others . . .
C) Understands how my own work has an effect on profits . . .
D) Absorbs relevant facts quickly . . .

For the Co-op, applicants are given short scenarios and then asked to select the most appropriate action. For example:
You notice that customers are starting to comment on the lack of variety of sandwiches available at lunchtime. Do you?

A) Speak to the person responsible for ordering sandwiches to make them aware of the customers' comments
B) Highlight the comments to your manager
C) Approach the customers to identify what additional varieties they would like to see then speak to the person who places the orders
D) Leave a note for your colleague by the computer for when they place the next order

You can either be completely honest when taking these tests or you can try to identify the personality traits the question is probably testing for and skew your answers accordingly. One risk is that you may get the balance wrong. For example, picking too many options that show you as methodical, accurate and someone who pays attention to detail when applying for an administrative post, may mean rejecting too many questions that show how creative or sociable you are. You may also be seen through and court their disapproval.

From the employer's point of view, the huge drawback to

personality tests must be that they often depend on your view of yourself. Whether or not someone selects all the options that show they love going to parties, talking to people and socializing so that they appear to be an extrovert and suitable for, let's say a sales post, these tests won't show if other people find them incredibly boring, patronizing or aggressive. Yet who hasn't backed out of a shop on occasion because an overzealous sales person has driven them away with inane chatter or a heavy sell?

Ability and reasoning tests

For fairness, these tests are conducted in a standardized way, rather like an examination, so that the instructions will be delivered using the same rubric each time, and they will have a set time limit. They usually offer a number of answers for each question where only one is correct and, apart from mental arithmetic, the right answer can often be worked out if you understand the underlying rules.

Numerical Aptitude or Reasoning Tests

They may include finding a missing number (or character) in a series; calculating percentages based on tables of data or graphs; mental arithmetic; estimations or interpreting figures after being given a series of statements.

Simple examples:

1   What is the next letter in the series ABBCDD?
    Answer: E (First letter of alphabet followed by two second letters, third letter of alphabet followed by two fourth letters, so the missing one must be the fifth letter of the alphabet)

2   What is the next number in the series 12, 24, 48?
    Answer: 96 (Each number is the previous one multiplied by 2)

3   48 + 13 = 16 + ? Choose from: 38, 41, 45, 56, 61
    Answer: 45 (48 + 13 = 61, which is the same as 16 + 45)

4   Estimate 45% of 382   Choose from 150, 170, 190, 210, 220
    Answer = 170 (The exact figure is 171.9)

5   Four out of eight motorists will be breathalysed in a police
    survey. How many motorists will be checked out of 250?
    Choose from 200, 180, 175, 125, 50
    Answer: 125 (4 out of 8 = 4/8 = ½)

Verbal Aptitude or Reasoning Tests
These may test your vocabulary, use of English and spelling or your
comprehension and logic by asking a series of questions based on a
given passage of text. In these tests you often have to select one of
three options: the statement is true, false or you cannot say.
    Simple examples:

1   Select the correct spelling: committee, comitee, comittee, com-
    mitee (Answer: committee)
2   Hear is to Listen as Touch is to . . .? (Answer: Feel)
3   Select the word that fits best with Milk, Cheese and Yoghurt from
    Juice, Water, Cream, Beer, Wine. (Answer: Cream as it is the only
    dairy product)

Abstract or Diagrammatical Aptitude (Inductive Reasoning) Tests
These often consist of a series of diagrams and you have to select
the next one in the series from five or so alternatives. Usually there
are one or two rules to apply so that you can predict what the next
diagram should show, e.g. a certain shape moves clockwise round
another, an arrow changes direction or alternative diagrams are
identical. Sometimes the same shape changes size or colour, or a
horizontal or vertical line is added or removed.
    Simple example: What will diagram 5 show?

Answer: A circle alone. The repeating pattern is 1. Circle in square. 2. Circle alone 3. Square alone. This is repeated with 4. Circle in square and so Circle alone must be the next diagram.

Clerical Data Checking

For many clerical and supervisory jobs, checking for errors can be important and so you may be offered a test that checks your ability to pick out matching data items or find missing entries.

For example: Pick out the two identical codes from the following five:

1   xLWpp4X
2   xLwPp4x
3   xLWpp4X
4   xLWpg4X
5   XLWPp4X

(Answer: 1 and 3)

Practice

If you know you are going to be asked to an assessment centre or to take some tests, you might like to ask your careers service if they can offer any mock tests. In particular, practising giving five-minute presentations on any subject to friends or family will help if you get particularly nervous in these situations.

For psychometric tests, it is a very good idea to familiarize yourself with the format and types of questions. You can read through one of the many books on the topic, including a number published by How To Books written by Andrea Shavick, or find examples of free tests that you can take online, e.g. at practicetests.cubiks.com, www.psychometric-success.com, www.kent.ac.uk/careers/psychotests.htm or www.shldirect.com/example_questions.html.

ACCEPTING THE JOB

If you are fortunate enough to be offered a job, you might think there would be no problems. But what if some of the features of the job don't appeal?

Even if there are no obvious alternative jobs on the horizon, taking a job that you don't want can be the wrong thing to do.

The answer is to carry out an evaluation exercise. At its simplest, this means noting down all the pros and cons and weighing them so that you end up with a final decision.

If one or two changes would make the difference between accepting and rejecting the job offer, there is also the option to try to negotiate a better deal with the employer. All they can say is no!

Here are ten aspects you might need to consider:

➤ **Day-to-day tasks** – will they be interesting, enjoyable or challenging enough, and is the situation likely to change soon?

➤ **Salary, now and for the future** – is it reasonable and will it give you the life you want?

➤ **Career development** – are there enough opportunities with this employer or in this field?

➤ **Colleagues** – will you enjoy working with this group of people or will you be lonely or uncomfortable?

➤ **Location** – do you like the environment and do you have to travel far to work?

➤ **Training** – is this good quality and will you get useful qualifications at the end?

➤ **Effect on quality of life** – will the job demand too many hours or too much travel and will it suit your lifestyle?

➤ **Security** – is this a full-time, permanent job or only short-term or temporary?

➤ **Status** – is this a job you would be proud to tell people you do, or is it too low-level or unattractive?

➤ **The organization/sector** – is it going places, a market leader or is it stagnating or showing negative growth?

If this post is your second choice and you are still hoping to hear from your first choice, holding out for a better or more attractive offer is risky. The current offer is unlikely to be kept open for long and you need to think about the consequences if you don't get the other job and end up with neither of them.

Depending on where you are in the process, you might want to ring up your preferred employer and find out if you are being considered seriously. If they cannot or will not tell you, the most sensible decision might be to take this job and then see how you feel about a move in six to twelve months' time. You would at least be applying from within a job rather than, possibly, as an unemployed graduate.

NO JOB OFFERS

If you have had several interviews but no job offers, there are a number of possible reasons:

1 Too many other applicants with better qualifications or experience
2 They have had to cut back on the numbers they could take
3 Poor interview technique that you were aware of at the time
4 Poor interview technique you hadn't identified
5 Lack of chemistry between you and the recruiter – a personal issue that is unlikely to be repeated often

If you were close to receiving an offer, it may just be a matter of time before you do get a job. Certainly if you could tell that some of your answers were weak or badly received, you can work on them before the next interview.

If you get too nervous, or don't know how to improve your

technique, you may need to seek help. Go to your careers service and see what advice they can give you, or take a presentation or public-speaking course if you think that would help you and boost your confidence.

If it was simply a lack of preparation – learn the lesson and do better next time.

COPING WITH UNEMPLOYMENT

It is quite possible that you will be unemployed at some stage, and many graduates find it takes time to find a first or permanent job, rather than a temporary position based around the busy Christmas period when retailers want staff.

If you have worries about finance and accommodation and need help sorting things out, these will obviously be your first priorities and there are agencies, including the Citizens Advice Bureau, to help you. For advice about Job Seekers Allowance or Universal Credits, for example, go to the Government website www.gov.uk/browse/benefits.

If you are one of a large number of students able to live at home who may not be eligible for benefits, then lying in bed all day, socializing or even spending every hour slogging round the streets with your CV should not be the only things you do.

Spend your time constructively:

- It is common to feel depressed after graduating as you may well find your whole way of life has changed and, if you are now back at home, you could be missing the presence of lots of other young people. If you are unable to get support from networking, friends or family and feel you cannot cope, try to find help as soon as possible. The best place to start is probably your GP.

- Many university careers services, councils or community groups have helped set up Job Clubs and there are several aimed at graduates, including in York, Sheffield and Teesside. Search the internet for your nearest group.

▪ Improve your transferable skills by taking a course, reading a self-help manual, volunteering or getting family or friends to help you.

▪ Find out more about the sectors or jobs of interest by working voluntarily or visiting and asking questions.

▪ Gain work-related skills by working voluntarily or via work experience, ideally in a relevant organization but anywhere is useful. This is very often the way people find out about an actual vacancy.

▪ Improve your qualifications if there are colleges or online courses open to you, especially if you want to work in a competitive industry or sector where many people will already have relevant vocational qualifications.

▪ Take up a leisure activity that provides a chance to develop specific or transferable skills, e.g. communication, numeracy, IT literacy, problem-solving, leadership or working in a team.

▪ Network in any way you can.

▪ Spend time setting up a small business/designing your own website/selling home-made items/offering tuition etc. – all things to show enterprise, initiative and develop your skills.

▪ Take your covering letters or CV to a recruitment agency or careers adviser for a second opinion, in case there are areas for improvement.

▪ If you live in Northern Ireland, there is a programme known as the Business in the Community's Graduate Acceleration Programme (GAP), which offers twenty-six weeks on a work-placement scheme for unemployed graduates and includes a leadership and management qualification.

(For more detailed ideas, look at the suggestions in the Introduction for what to do before leaving university as many will be just as appropriate after you have graduated.)

SUMMARY

1 Think up concrete examples of when you have used particular skills so you can talk through them at the interview.

2 Always have a couple of questions to ask at the end.

3 Telephone interviews are quite common so prepare just as carefully for these.

4 Do as much practise as you can before an assessment centre so you are confident you can carry out the tasks and are prepared for the tests.

5 If you don't have any job offers, make constructive use of your time or seek help if you are not coping.

STEP 7

CHANGING DIRECTION

If you have so far failed to find work in the conventional way, or if you want to do something different, there are many alternative approaches to life after university, apart from going into further education. This section of the book covers:

➤ Becoming self-employed. There are four main routes into self-employment:

1 Setting up a business – either as a sole trader or after taking on employees or joining other partners, you could provide a range of goods and services locally, nationally or worldwide.

2 Working freelance – this is where you don't have a business as such but offer your services to organizations for a set fee or on a fixed contract. At the end of each contract, you need to find new assignments.

3 Taking on a franchise – here you buy an ongoing business with a well-known brand name and then run the outlet yourself.

4 Providing other services or goods that you are paid for direct.

➤ Going abroad

➤ Alternative lifestyle

➤ Supporting the community

SELF-EMPLOYMENT

This means working for yourself rather than an employer so that you are responsible for paying your own taxes and contributions, like national insurance, but, within limits, have the freedom to work how and when you like. Clearly once you set up a business or take on a contract, you need to meet the needs of your clients or customers, but to a certain extent you can turn down work that doesn't appeal and you are always ultimately in charge of what you do.

The disadvantages include owing money if you borrowed and the business then fails, not being paid for holidays or illness unless you take out your own private insurance, often having to work far harder than if you were employed – especially at the start of a new venture – and being at far greater risk than when working for someone else.

You can set up very easily if you have a good idea and appropriate skills, but you may prefer to take a business course or get advice first. Many careers services offer 'Start Your Own Business' courses in the summer and the Government has help for the unemployed. Visit their website at www.gov.uk/moving-from-benefits-to-work/starting-your-own-business to see if you qualify for any support.

Some useful tasks might include:

➢ Looking into start-up finance sources, e.g. friends and family, applying for a grant or a bank loan, winning a prize or finding an investor such as a venture capital company or business 'angel'

➢ Joining a professional body – they often have self-employment sections and you can get advice or network with others

➢ Talking to other self-employed people about how they started and what problems they had to overcome

Set up a business

I probably don't need to point out the advantages of running your own business, but here are a few reminders. You will:

➤ Not have to apply for a job
➤ Be able to live where you like (bar constraints like transport or customer base)
➤ Be your own boss
➤ Be able to take the business where you want
➤ Make a contribution to society and the economy
➤ Be free to maintain your own values

EXAMPLE

Jenny Dawson, a Maths and Economics graduate who previously worked at a hedge fund, set up Rubies in the Rubble to make chutneys and jam from surplus food. The company employs individuals who are struggling to get back into work and tackles a culture of excessive waste by using otherwise discarded fruit and vegetables.

It all depends on the actual business whether you would need help or financial assistance. Some businesses will require premises such as a factory, kitchen or workshop, whereas for others it may be quite possible to run them from home. For some businesses you will need to employ people straight away but for others you could do all the work on your own. Here are a few examples of the wide range of businesses you might set up:

- **Craftwork** – making jewellery, greetings cards, baskets or knitting or sewing socks, bags or clothes and selling them via your own website, Etsy or eBay. You might do all the work yourself or employ outworkers to make some of your goods in their own homes.

- **Cooking** – you could make home-made bread, cakes or jams and sell them on a market stall or supply local shops, or you could run a small catering business where you visited and cooked on clients' premises or took your cooked food with you. Again, you could start in your own kitchen and possibly employ one or two others to help you.

- **Repairs** – if you had a van you could offer a mobile repair service to people in their own homes, taking all your tools and equipment with you, or you could rent premises and attract customers there.

- **Tuition** – if you offered music, languages, art, computing or other training, you could visit people in their own homes or businesses, get clients to come to your home or hire a studio or workshop.

- **Web design services** – this is a common business to run entirely from home as most communication would be online and you would just need to buy or hire suitable software or other tools.

- **Health specialists** such as sports therapists, chiropodists, osteopaths or counsellors are often self-employed and work from home, hire appropriate premises or rent rooms in health centres.

Whatever business you decide to set up, you will usually need to think up a good name, register a domain and set up a website; understand and use both off and online advertising; and be aware of ramifications related to employment law, tax and pension issues, health and safety and liability and employer insurance.

One of the skills you will need will be an ability to multitask. Until you have an established business, you will probably be responsible for everything including finance, marketing, sales, personnel, manufacturing and delivery.

For advice and support, check if your university has an Enterprise Unit and contact your local Business Link (staffed by experienced managers who offer advice to new businesses), the NCEE (the National Centre for Entrepreneurship in Education) that supports graduate enterprise at www.ncee.org.uk, or a National Enterprise Network adviser, e.g. at www.nationalenterprisenetwork.org.

If you are between the ages of eighteen and thirty and graduated over six months ago, the Princes Trust at www.princes-trust.org.uk offers a support programme, grants and courses to those who are unemployed and thinking of setting up a business. In Scotland, you can get in touch with First Port at www.firstport.org.uk.

If you are interested in a one-year placement, the NEF (National Enterprise Foundation) selects up to thirty of the UK's 'brightest, most entrepreneurially minded people each year to join their paid programme'. Go to www.brightnetwork.co.uk/new-entrepreneurs-foundation to learn more and find out how to apply. Applications for the following year's programme open each November.

ACTIVITY 40

1   Are you interested in setting up a business?

2   Start putting down your ideas for what this might be and what you need to do to get started.

3   Discuss your ideas with one of the advisory bodies mentioned above.

Freelancing

Anyone can become a freelance worker (an independent profes-sional) as you just apply for projects or short-term contracts to work on, rather than being employed in a single job. Freelancers work in a wide variety of fields, but are particularly prevalent in the digital, media and technology sectors. They are popular with employers because they are only taken on for the duration of the project, rather than being on the books when business is poor. Examples of freelancing opportunities include:

- Writing, editing and proof-reading
- Translating
- Web developing
- Training
- Broadcasting
- Film and video-making
- Marketing
- Software analysis
- Production assistant
- Graphic design
- Bookkeeping
- Events organizing

The advantages of this way of working include the flexibility to work as and when you want to and the variety of work as well as organizations you can work for, but you cannot rely on a regular income and will have to spend quite a bit of time looking for the next project. You will also have to be very organized, especially if juggling a number of projects at the same time, and widen your skills base so you can always meet your clients' demands.

The ideal way to find a job is word of mouth or through contacts and networks, but there are also a large number of vacancy websites advertising outsourced or freelance jobs. Unfortunately, some are based on you bidding for the job and so you have to be careful not to offer to work for too low a fee.

One helpful website is Student Gems at www.studentgems.com, which offers projects to students and graduates looking for temporary or short-term work.

ACTIVITY 41

1 Do you have any skills you feel you could offer straight away to someone looking for a freelance worker?

2 If you would like to find freelance work, register at Student Gems or look at the various freelance vacancy websites to see if any of the jobs appeal or you feel you could do them.

Franchises

Some of the most well-known companies in the UK are built on the franchise model, and they include:

- Subway
- McDonald's
- Dunkin' Donuts
- Starbucks
- Pizza Hut
- Clarks shoes
- Holiday Inn
- Shell Retail

Other types of franchise business include cleaning companies, fitness clubs, garden maintenance, estate agents, tuition services, recruitment agencies, printers, pubs and pet products.

This is not an easy business for a new graduate as so much money is needed at the start and there are many legal implications, but it may appeal to those of you looking for a ready-made business opportunity.

Once you have bought the franchise (which means the licence to trade), the company (franchisor) often provides training, management expertise and national marketing as well as raw materials and equipment. You have to pay them part of your profits, but keep the rest and – as long as you stick to the basic model, maintain standards and agree to the pricing set by the franchisor – can choose the way to develop your business. The initial cost can be many hundreds of thousands of pounds, but the business is up and running, well known and often has an established geographical area to trade in.

You will also be taking advantage of the company's national recognition and advertising, and customer loyalty to the brand.

To find out more about franchises, visit the British Franchise Association website at www.thebfa.org.

Other self-employment options

For many professions, particularly in the creative arts such as acting, film directing, book writing, teaching or painting, you are most likely to be self-employed and so will need to spend quite a bit of time seeking paid work or selling your products or services.

To find outlets, you can:

➤ Pitch projects, e.g. to publishers

➤ Audition for parts

➤ Sell online, e.g. via your own website

➤ Take products to exhibitions and conferences

➤ Hold your own exhibitions

➤ Network amongst family and friends

➤ Hire space or rent rooms and put up posters

➤ Advertise through local newspapers and radio

ACTIVITY 42

1   Do you have any ideas for self-employment?

2   Make a list of what you would need to do to make money from your idea.

3   Set a goal for your first action and try to follow this through.

GOING ABROAD

Although a gap year is very common before, during or after studying for a degree, it is usually seen as a short-term experience. You can also view living and working overseas as a real alternative to looking for work in the UK. There is, of course, also the option to go and study at a university overseas or find an international employer.

A common approach is to simply take off independently and travel round the world, finding seasonal and other temporary jobs where you can. If you just want time to think about your options, one organization with lots of suggestions for taking a gap year is the Year Out Group, so visit their website at www.yearoutgroup.org to read about what is available. There is also BUNAC at bunac.org/uk, which has information about volunteering and paid work overseas. When looking for overseas opportunities, World Service Enquiry at www.wse.org.uk is another place that provides information and careers advice to anyone wanting to spend time abroad.

The range of opportunities you might consider, especially if you want to organize a placement first rather than simply looking for jobs in any country you visit, include:

➢ Study overseas

➢ Voluntary work

➢ Teaching English as a foreign language

➢ Working at summer camps and activity centres

➢ Overseas development work

Study overseas

A number of organizations offer advice and help on studying overseas, and it is worth exploring some of these. They include scholarships or other help to go to the USA (www.fulbright.org.uk/study-in-the-usa), the Commonwealth (www.cscuk.dfid.gov) and Australia (www.idp.com/idp-student-placement.aspx). There are also many short courses or MAs across the world that you could take, and a useful source of information is provided by www.thecompleteuniversityguide.co.uk/international/funding-overseas-study. Unlike studying in the UK, in a non-English speaking country you will also be learning and practising a different language.

A different type of scholarship is provided each year by Rotary International – see www.ribi.org/what-we-do/scholarships-and-exchanges/ambassadorial-scholarships. These are one-year opportunities to study at an international university in one of the following areas:

➤ Peace Studies and Conflict Resolution

➤ Maternal and Child Health

➤ Disease Prevention and Treatment

➤ Water and Sanitation

➤ Education and Literacy

➤ Community and Economic Development

Voluntary work

The most well-known organization offering graduates a structured overseas experience together with living costs is VSO – Voluntary Service Overseas (see www.vso.org.uk). For those aged eighteen to twenty-five without work experience, you would only be offered a three-month placement on the government-funded International Citizen Service (ICS) programme, but after that you could build on your overseas experience and do something entirely different.

Once you have two years' experience and relevant qualifications, you can work for VSO as a specialist, adviser or trainer in one of a wide variety of fields, such as agriculture, horticulture, fund-raising, marketing, health, laboratory work, therapy, engineering, management, tourism, IT or teaching.

The United Nations Refugee Agency (UNHCR) offers volunteering posts and also internships that last two to six months. Full details are available at www.unhcr.org.

An organization active in most universities is AIESEC. This arranges international exchanges where you can work or volunteer and help organize programmes for other students. Details are available at www.aiesec.co.uk. According to their publicity, 'students and recent graduates develop their leadership skills by running and participating in an international exchange program'.

A different body offering opportunities abroad is Projects Abroad at www.projects-abroad.co.uk/why-projects-abroad/recent-graduates. They can offer work with children, helping teach, coach or look after those in care, as well as the usual range of business, language, conservation, finance, building or IT activities. Alternatively, the Raleigh Graduate Bursary Award for Volunteering Overseas offers sixty bursaries on a Raleigh expedition to Costa Rica and Nicaragua, Borneo or India. Details can be found at www.raleighinternational. org/what-we-do/raleigh-expeditions/aged-17-24. You would have to find some of the cost yourself, usually through fund-raising activities, and they are also involved in the ICS scheme.

If you are interested in conservation, Frontier at www.frontier. ac.uk provides details of a range of projects that you could become involved in, as well as other overseas work like teaching English or even journalism internships.

Many professional bodies provide information on overseas work or placements where you would use your specialist skills directly. For example, if you have a veterinary degree, you probably know about the overseas opportunities there are, but find out more at the British Veterinary Association's website at www.bva.co.uk/overseas/ Overseas_experiences.aspx.

Teaching English (TEFL)

To teach English as a foreign language abroad (or to teach English to foreigners in the UK, where it is known as TESOL – teaching English to speakers of other languages), you need to gain appropriate teaching qualifications. There are a huge number of these short courses around, so look for accreditation by an outside body such as a UK university. The highest qualification is the DELTA (Diploma in English Language Teaching for Adults), but there is also a certificate course CELTA available that is accepted widely overseas.

Courses can be costly (over £1,000 for a four-week course), but one option is to go and stay in a low-cost country and train there. Links to courses in some countries can be found at www.cactustefl.com/get_started/budget.php, and Cactus also offers its own scholarship each year.

For unemployed graduates, the British Council offers subsidies (perhaps half the cost) to 'successful applicants to study an intensive or part-time Trinity CertTESOL or Cambridge CELTA course at a UK training centre'. Find details of the scheme at englishagenda.britishcouncil.org/english-teaching-graduate-scheme.

Several organizations will provide training and then find places for you in Japan, China or elsewhere, or will offer help after you have gained your teaching qualifications separately. Here are a few organizations to explore further: www.jet-uk.org for placements in Japan; www.lovetefl.com/recruiters that offers, amongst other things, a six-month China internship programme; www.tefl.com, which is a portal for various organizations offering vacancies; www.ttmadrid.com, running training courses in Spain; www.teflworldwideprague.com, offering training courses and then work in Prague, and www.discovereltvietnam.com, which finds jobs in Vietnam.

Once you have a couple of years' teaching experience, the British Council regularly lists vacancies on their website at jobs.britishcouncil.org.

Summer camps

If you don't want to teach English, you might be interested in helping on an overseas summer camp or at an activity centre. The most well-known company offering graduates a chance to do this at one of their twenty-four centres in France and Spain as well as the UK is PGL – details at www.pgl.co.uk. According to their website, 'we have job vacancies for Activity Instructors, Watersports Instructors, Catering jobs, Housekeeping jobs and many more! Fantastic work and training opportunities for careers in the outdoors, gap year jobs, seasonal jobs and career breaks. Earn while you learn: we offer Apprenticeships, NVQs, training and nationally recognized qualification opportunities to our staff team to help you realise your potential.'

For work in the USA, organizations involved include Camp America, AmeriCamp, Wildpacks and Camp Leaders. If you prefer other parts of the world, work supervising children in holiday resorts and hotels is often available and one company to contact about vacancies is In2Action at www.in2action.co.uk.

Overseas development

If you go to WSE's work page at www.wse.org.uk/work/job.htm you will find a list of NGOs (Non Governmental Organizations) and other international bodies together with links to their vacancy details. They include well-known names such as Medair, Oxfam, British Red Cross, World Health Organization and the World Bank. You may be able to work with them having just a first degree, but they will expect to see volunteering or overseas experience.

ALTERNATIVE LIFESTYLES

There are different ways of living and you might prefer to drop out of the rat race completely, growing your own food and becoming self-sufficient, or joining with other like-minded people to set up a cooperative or commune where you live and support each other through selling or bartering with what you make and grow.

There is advice on a range of alternative lifestyles on the Web. Go to Diggers and Dreamers at www.diggersanddreamers.org.uk for a guide to communal living, or find out more about downsizing at www.downsizer.net and self-sufficiency at www.viableselfsufficiency.co.uk and www.lowcostliving.co.uk.

A range of alternative careers you might never have considered, from busking to mortuary technician, burlesque, lookalike or film extra, can be found at www.mookychick.co.uk/how-to/fun-alternative-jobs, and it is also worth reading the BBC pages at news.bbc.co.uk/1/hi/talking_point/4169490.stm which highlight examples of some very unusual jobs too.

SUPPORTING THE COMMUNITY

There are many volunteering opportunities in the UK that you can contribute to on a long-term or regular basis. Organizations such as TimeBank at www.timebanking.org let you type in your town or postcode and find mentoring roles, and www.csv.org.uk/volunteering and www.volunteering.org.uk are just two of the many bodies that can help you locate a wide range of voluntary experiences from helping with animal welfare to conservation or care. There are also a number of summer camps organized in the UK as well as overseas, and companies to contact include PGL, Supercamps and Camp Beaumont. Links to many organizations can be found at www.student-jobs.co.uk.

If you like music, the music festivals always need volunteer helpers to act as stewards and you get into the venues free and may even earn a small hourly wage. Go to individual festival websites or visit www.oxfam.org.uk/get-involved/festivals or ndssltd.co.uk/employment as they offer jobs at some of the biggest festivals including Bestival, Reading, Glastonbury and Download.

If you are political, concerned about aspects of life in Britain or feel strongly about any issues like airports, roads or carbon emissions, there are roles for those interested or skilled in fund-raising, producing publicity material, organizing events or carrying out office work. You could find jobs with political parties, charities or campaigning organizations. There are also many environmental groups that need people to clear canals or help maintain woodland. A couple of websites to look at are www.charityjob.co.uk/jobs/

Campaigning and the South-west London Environmental Group www.swlen.org.uk/looking-for-a-group.

Most of the roles will be unpaid, although charities do employ some paid staff so there is the possibility of staying on with a charity you volunteer with and eventually finding a paid position. As a volunteer still free to work, you may need to look for a job or series of temporary positions to keep you going.

CONCLUSION

Even if this book has not helped you decide conclusively about what to do with your life, I hope it has given you lots of ideas and offered you a glimpse of the wide range of possibilities open to you.

There are jobs out there, but you may need to think laterally or do something really original or against your normal instincts in order to get the chance to make your case. There are also alternatives to conventional jobs that may suit your current circumstances or goals.

Perhaps the one lesson it is worth emphasizing is how important it may be to develop your networking skills. People are usually happy to help and picking the brains of friends, family, colleagues, academics, acquaintances and new contacts you make through online or local networks may turn out to be the best way of finding a job after university and certainly a good way to get support and advice.

SUMMARY

1 Becoming self-employed may be as satisfying as working for an employer.

2 There are many opportunities for graduates overseas whether you study, work or volunteer.

3 If it appeals, you might want to consider an alternative lifestyle such as self-sufficiency or communal living.

4 Voluntary work in the UK can be very satisfying for people who want to make a contribution and may be available on a short-term, regular or long-term basis.

INDEX